MW00799308

# Panorama of the Old Testament

**Stephen J. Binz**

with Little Rock Scripture Study staff

Little Rock
Scripture Study

*A ministry of the Diocese of Little Rock*
*in partnership with Liturgical Press*

*Nihil obstat* for the commentary text by Stephen J. Binz: Reverend Robert Harren, J.C.L., *Censor deputatis*. *Imprimatur* for the commentary text by Stephen J. Binz: ✠ Most Reverend Donald J. Kettler, J.C.L., Bishop of Saint Cloud, Minnesota, June 7, 2016.

Cover design by Ann Blattner. Interior art by Ned Bustard.

Scripture texts in this work are taken from the *New American Bible, revised edition* © 2010, 1991, 1986, 1970 Confraternity of Christian Doctrine, Washington, D.C. and are used by permission of the copyright owner. All Rights Reserved. No part of the New American Bible may be reproduced in any form without permission in writing from the copyright owner.

Excerpt from the English translation of the *Catechism of the Catholic Church* for use in the United States of America copyright © 1994, United States Catholic Conference, Inc.—Libreria Editrice Vaticana. English translation of the *Catechism of the Catholic Church: Modifications from the Editio Typica* copyright © 1997, United States Catholic Conference, Inc.—Libreria Editrice Vaticana. Used with Permission.

 This symbol indicates material that was created by Little Rock Scripture Study to supplement the biblical text and commentary. Some of these inserts first appeared in *Panorama of the Bible: Old Testament* or in the *Little Rock Catholic Study Bible*; others were created specifically for this book by Amy Ekeh.

Commentary by Stephen J. Binz, © 2016, 2018 by Order of Saint Benedict, Collegeville, Minnesota. All rights reserved. No part of this book may be used or reproduced in any manner whatsoever, except brief quotations in reviews, without written permission of Liturgical Press, Saint John's Abbey, PO Box 7500, Collegeville, MN 56321-7500. Printed in the United States of America.

Inserts adapted from *Little Rock Catholic Study Bible*, © 2011 by Little Rock Scripture Study, Little Rock, Arkansas; additional inserts, prayers, and study questions by Little Rock Scripture Study staff, © 2018 by Little Rock Scripture Study. All rights reserved. No part of this book may be reproduced in any form or by any means without the written permission of the copyright holder. Published by Liturgical Press, Collegeville, Minnesota 56321. Printed in the United States of America.

1     2     3     4     5     6     7     8     9

**Library of Congress Cataloging-in-Publication Data**

Names: Binz, Stephen J., 1955– author.
Title: Panorama of the Old Testament / Stephen J. Binz, with Little Rock Scripture Study staff.
Description: Collegeville, Minnesota : Liturgical Press, 2018. | Series: Little Rock Scripture study | "Little Rock Scripture Study, a ministry of the Diocese of Little Rock, in partnership with Liturgical Press."
Identifiers: LCCN 2018028650 (print) | LCCN 2018047301 (ebook) | ISBN 9780814663974 (ebook) | ISBN 9780814663721
Subjects: LCSH: Bible. Old Testament—Textbooks.
Classification: LCC BS1194 (ebook) | LCC BS1194 .B53 2018 (print) | DDC 221.6—dc23
LC record available at https://lccn.loc.gov/2018028650

Office of the Bishop

**DIOCESE OF LITTLE ROCK**

2500 North Tyler Street • P.O. Box 7565 • Little Rock, Arkansas 72217 • (501) 664 0340  Fax (501) 664-6304

Dear Friends,

   The Bible is a gift of God to the church, the people gathered around the world throughout the ages in the name of Christ. God uses this sacred writing to continue to speak to us in all times and places.

   I encourage you to make it your own by dedicated prayer and study with others and on your own. Little Rock Scripture Study is a ministry of the Catholic Diocese of Little Rock. It provides the tools you need to faithfully understand what you are reading, to appreciate its meaning for you and for our world, and to guide you in a way that will deepen your own ability to respond to God's call.

   It is my hope that the Word of God will empower you as Christians to live a life worthy of your call as a child of God.


Sincerely in Christ,

✠ Anthony B. Taylor
Bishop of Little Rock

# TABLE OF CONTENTS

Wrap-up lectures are available for each lesson at no charge. The link to these free lectures is LittleRockScripture.org/Lectures/PanoramaOldTestament.

# Welcome

The Bible is at the heart of what it means to be a Christian. It is the Spirit-inspired word of God for us. It reveals to us the God who created, redeemed, and guides us still. It speaks to us personally and as a church. It forms the basis of our public liturgical life and our private prayer lives. It urges us to live worthily and justly, to love tenderly and wholeheartedly, and to be a part of building God's kingdom here on earth.

Though it was written a long time ago, in the context of a very different culture, the Bible is no relic of the past. Catholic biblical scholarship is among the best in the world, and in our time and place, we have unprecedented access to it. By making use of solid scholarship, we can discover much about the ancient culture and religious practices that shaped those who wrote the various books of the Bible. With these insights, and by praying with the words of Scripture, we allow the words and images to shape us as disciples. By sharing our journey of faithful listening to God's word with others, we have the opportunity to be stretched in our understanding and to form communities of love and learning. Ultimately, studying and praying with God's word deepens our relationship with Christ.

## Panorama of the Old Testament

The resource you hold in your hands is divided into four lessons. Each lesson involves personal prayer and study using this book *and* the experience of group prayer, discussion, and wrap-up lecture.

If you are using this resource in the context of a small group, we suggest that you meet four times, discussing one lesson per meeting. Allow about 90 minutes for the small group gathering. Small groups function best with eight to twelve people to ensure good group dynamics and allow all to participate as they wish.

WHAT MATERIALS WILL YOU USE?

The materials in this book include:

- Commentary by Stephen J. Binz, which has also been published separately as *Panorama of the Bible: Old Testament* (Liturgical Press).

- Occasional inserts ◉ highlighting elements of the Old Testament. Some of these appear also in the *Little Rock*

*Catholic Study Bible* while others are supplied by staff writers.

- Questions for study, reflection, and discussion at the end of each lesson.

- Opening and closing prayers for each lesson, as well as other prayer forms available in the closing pages of the book.

In addition, there are wrap-up lectures available for each lesson. Your group may choose to purchase a DVD containing these lectures or make use of the audio or video lectures online at no charge. The link to these free lectures is: LittleRockScripture.org/Lectures/PanoramaOldTestament. Of course, if your group has access to qualified speakers, you may choose to have live presentations.

Each person will need a current translation of the Bible. We recommend the *Little Rock Catholic Study Bible*, which makes use of the New American Bible, Revised Edition. Other translations, such as the New Jerusalem Bible or the New Revised Standard Version: Catholic Edition, would also work well.

## HOW WILL YOU USE THESE MATERIALS?

### Prepare in advance

Using Lesson One as an example:

- Begin with a simple prayer like the one found on page 11.

- Read the assigned material in the printed book for Lesson One (pages 12–13) so that you are prepared for the weekly small group session. You may do this assignment by reading a portion over a period of several days (effective and manageable) or by preparing all at once (more challenging).

- Answer the questions, Exploring Lesson One, found at the end of the assigned reading, pages 32–34.

- Use the Closing Prayer on page 35 when you complete your study. This prayer may be used again when you meet with the group.

### Meet with your small group

- After introductions and greetings, allow time for prayer (about 5 minutes) as you begin the group session. You may use the prayer found on page 11 (also used by individuals in their preparation) or use a prayer of your choosing.

- Spend about 45–50 minutes discussing the responses to the questions that were prepared in advance. You may also develop your discussion further by responding to questions and interests that arise during the discussion and faith-sharing itself.

- Close the discussion and faith-sharing with prayer, about 5–10 minutes. You may use the Closing Prayer at the end of each lesson or one of your choosing at the end of the book. It is important to allow people to pray for personal and community needs and to give thanks for how God is moving in your lives.

- Listen to or view the wrap-up lecture associated with each lesson (15–20 minutes). You may watch the lecture online, use a DVD, or provide a live lecture by a qualified local speaker. This lecture provides a common focus for the group and reinforces insights from each lesson. You may view the lecture together at the end of the session or, if your group runs out of time, you may invite group members to watch the lecture on their own time after the discussion.

*Above all, be aware that the Holy Spirit is moving within and among you.*

# Panorama of the Old Testament

## LESSON ONE

### The Pentateuch

Begin your personal study and group discussion with a simple and sincere prayer such as:

*Prayer*

*Loving God, you liberated your people and led them to the Promised Land. Liberate our minds and hearts as we study your word, that we may live joyfully as your faithful people.*

Read the Preface on pages 12–13, and pages 14–31, Lesson One.

Respond to the questions on pages 32–34, Exploring Lesson One.

The Closing Prayer on page 35 is for your personal use and may be used at the end of group discussion.

# PREFACE

People in every culture seem to tell their story around the table. One of my fond memories of childhood is Sunday dinner at my grandparent's house. Our whole family—aunts, uncles, and cousins—would gather at the table for the meal, and my grandparents would tell stories of the past. Looking back on that experience helps me to realize that the narratives they told around the table are an important part of who I am. At the family dinner I realized how our family came to be, where I fit into the story, and I learned the family traditions that I would continue and reshape in my own life.

The family of God tells our story at the table, too. For ancient Israelites, the Passover meal was one way they passed on the narrative of salvation: how they were slaves and how God delivered them, led them through the trials of the wilderness, and brought them into a land where they could live as a free people. For disciples of Jesus, the Eucharist is that sacred meal where the past is narrated and where we join our lives to that story of salvation around the table.

Every time we pick up the Bible and read, we are either preparing ourselves for the family meal or savoring our memories of the table. The Bible is like our family album, like a chest containing old family treasures. It is the literature of the people of God, the book of the church. When we reflect on the words of Scripture, either with others or in quiet solitude, we learn who we are, where we come from, and where we are going. We discover the truths that keep our family of faith together, and we learn what it means to live as a member of that family.

We open the Bible to hear our story. The history of salvation includes what God has done in the past, as well as what God is doing for us now, and what God will do in the future. But sometimes we miss the big picture. We often know individual characters and events in the great narrative of God and humanity, but we fail to comprehend how the whole Bible fits together. Focusing exclusively on parts of the story, we miss the overall plot and how the various narrative threads intertwine to tie together God's wondrous plan.

The Bible is a magnificent library of seventy-three books. But, more important, this wonderful variety of books forms one tradition and is one story of salvation. This one Bible, the essential library of the descendants of Abraham, is the book of the church. Although the Bible consists of many books and a variety of different types of literature, the whole Bible is the narrative of God's redemption of the world. Patriarchs and matriarchs, prophets, judges, kings, priests, apostles, and evangelists belong to this inspired book of life.

This biblical account of redemption encompasses the whole world and offers us God's intentions and desires, which give cohesion, meaning, and purpose to human life. It is the grand narrative that explains for us the way things are, how they came to be so, and what they will ultimately be. It begins with creation and ends with the renewal of all things in the new creation for which we are destined. And in between, it offers us an interpretation of the whole of human history. Learning to take a panoramic view of the Bible enables us to live in the narrative and discover the real story of which each of our lives is a part.

So this panorama of the Bible, presented in two volumes—one on the Old Testament and one on the New Testament—offers a bird's-eye view of the Bible. Like looking at a map before setting out on a journey, we will survey the Scriptures so that later in other studies we can explore the riches in each book of the Bible. There is not a book in the Bible that can be interpreted satisfactorily in isolation from the rest. The central themes that run throughout the whole of Scripture offer us the big picture through which we can appreciate the details more clearly.

These two volumes belong together. Together they express one unfolding drama. As St. Augustine wrote, "The New Testament lies hidden in the Old, and the Old Testament is unveiled in the New" (*On the Spirit and the Letter* 15.27). The Scriptures of Israel and the writings of the early church are both necessary for a full understanding of God's saving plan. They are both important for Christian readers because together they are the word of the Lord.

When we understand that the Bible is our literature, we can enter into the story personally and view our lives as participants in the grand narrative of salvation. So, as we review this panorama of the Bible, it will be the responsibility of each reader to continually ask the personal questions: How do I fit into this great story of God and humanity? How do I enter this narrative of salvation today? How is my life being shaped by this inspired literature and molded into the person I was created to be? The more we can understand the whole drama as one grand narrative of salvation and then find ourselves within that story, the better we will embody Scripture and become participants in the mission of God.

## ISRAEL'S BEGINNINGS

The Pentateuch is the first five books of the Bible: Genesis, Exodus, Leviticus, Numbers, and Deuteronomy. "Pentateuch" comes from the Greek meaning "five scrolls." In Hebrew, these books are known as the Torah, best translated as "teaching" or "instruction." The Torah forms the founding charter of Israel as a nation and as a religion. It contains many different forms of writing: poetry, legend, genealogy, law, and the epic history of the nation.

These books are attributed to Moses, which means that he is the central figure and the authority behind these books. In fact he appears in almost every chapter of the last four books. But the first book, that of Genesis, doesn't mention him at all. Rather it forms a preparation and preview of the central events to follow.

The Bible begins by setting the story of Israel's past within the framework of the wider context of the whole world. The first eleven chapters of Genesis attempt to answer some of life's most basic questions about the origins of the world, the meaning of good and evil, and God's plan for humanity.

### God's Desire for Creation

The whole sweep of the Bible—from its first book, Genesis, to its last book, Revelation—expresses God's desire to offer the fullness of life to the world. The opening two chapters narrate that God, "in the beginning," created "the heavens and the earth" (Gen 1–2). And the final two chapters relate that God is establishing "a new heaven and a new earth" (Rev 21–22). These chapters frame the entire biblical narrative of the world's salvation. The process that God desired from the beginning is fulfilled as all creation is perfected and glorified according to God's plan.

The opening chapters of Genesis present us with God's intended design for the earth. In the initial creation account of Genesis 1, God is pictured as creating all that exists. The account is organized like a typical week for the Hebrews—six days of work followed by the Sabbath of rest. The world is shown to be the work of the great artisan, working with creative skill, then relaxing to enjoy the work.

The first three days are depicted as days of separation: the light from the darkness, the sky from the water, and the water from the land. The next three days are shown as days of population: the sun, moon, and stars, the birds of the sky and the fish of the sea, and the animals and people to populate the land. Compared to the creation of a temple, we can say that the divine builder spends three days constructing the holy place and then three days furnishing it. And on the seventh day, God rests and honors this "very good" creation, blessing the seventh day and making it holy.

**Six Days of Creation**

| Day | Domain | Creatures | Day |
|-----|--------|-----------|-----|
| 1 | Day & Night | Sun, Moon & Stars | 4 |
| 2 | Sky & Water | Birds & Fishes | 5 |
| 3 | Dry Land | Animals & Humans | 6 |

All of the attention in this creation narrative is on God, the one uncreated reality. God alone is divine and eternal, so powerful that only the divine will causes creation to spring into being. God's word of command, the repeated "Let there be . . ." brings forth a world characterized by order and harmony. Only this God, the cause and source of all things, is worthy of worship.

The seven-day framework for God's creation, the formation of man and woman in the divine image, God's walking with them in the garden, and the forbidden tree of knowledge are all figurative expressions of what God most deeply desires for creation. God does not distance himself from creation, but rules over it in a deeply personal way. God makes the garden the place of divine dwelling with man and woman, and as they continue to multiply and fill the earth, God wishes the whole earth to be that divine dwelling place.

To read these stories as if they were simply historical information would diminish the richness of meaning and depth of truth contained within them. The writers are not writing as journalists, scientists, or historians would write. The stories presume the primitive worldview of the ancient Middle East. The earth they understood was a flat surface covered by a dome called the firmament, which let in the

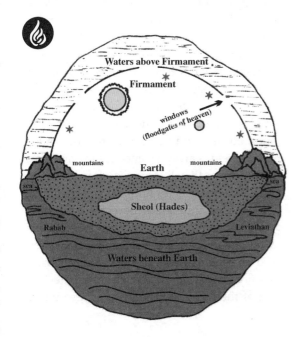

rain and the snow. The earth was elevated above the sea and the waters beneath the earth.

The Garden of Eden is described as a divine sanctuary where God is at home and lives in harmony with creation. Like ancient temples, it is entered through its east side where it is guarded by cherubim. God's command that the human being (Hebrew: ʾadam) "serve and care for" the garden are the same verbs used in later passages to describe the duties of Israel's priests in the tabernacle. So, human beings were designed by God to serve as priests in this garden-sanctuary with direct access to God.

Similarly, God's creation of man and woman in the "image of God" confers regal status upon them. In the ancient world of other cultures, the divine image was linked to kings. The royal ruler was believed to be the living image of the divine sovereign. In Israel, this regal status is confirmed as God gives the man and woman dominion over every living thing, appointing them to rule with divine care and justice over God's creation. As man and woman are fruitful and their descendants spread throughout the earth, they are to extend the reign of God throughout creation. So, God's original design for human beings is that they be royal rulers throughout the earth and a kingdom of priests.

Clearly, the creation accounts do not so much address the question of "how" the world came to be, as the more important question of "why" the world was created. They are a profound meditation on the meaning of creation. The ancient authors choose to pass on the truths that they have come to know in the form of stories, and these stories of creation are very successful attempts to express the essential truths about existence and life.

These stories have been honored for thousands of years because people have understood that they address some of the most profound and important questions of human life: What is our purpose? What is God like? What does God want us to be like?

Some of the essential truths taught by the creation account of Genesis 1 are these:

- There is one supreme God, unlike the multiple gods of other nations.

- God is the primary cause of all that exists.

- The sun and moon are not gods, as other religions believed, but part of God's creation.

- All creation is good, and people are the peak of that good creation.

- Men and women are equally made in the image of a loving God.

- Men and women are cocreators with God and stewards of the earth.

### God's Design Disrupted by Human Sin

A second creation story, which includes the story of sin, follows the first creation account. The editor of Genesis decided to include both of these creation stories because both had long been treasured within the community as expressing the truth about God and humanity.

In this second account of Genesis 2, God forms ʾadam from the ground (ʾadama), and breathes the divine breath into his nostrils to make him live. God then plants the Garden of Eden and places the man there. When God forms birds and animals from the ground, God presents them to the man for naming. But when none of them prove to be a suitable companion for the man, God builds a woman from the side of the man. When she is brought to the man, he recognizes that she is not from the ground like the animals but from his very self: "bone of my bones / and flesh of my flesh" (Gen 2:23). And like children, they feel no shame in their nakedness.

In both creation accounts, we see that human beings are made for God, for one another, and for the created world. As God's royal stewards and priests, we are responsible for developing the world in such a way that all creation gives God glory. But as the narrative continues, God's design is disrupted by the refusal of man and woman to live according to God's desire for creation. The cunning serpent, one of God's creatures, deceptively distorts God's words and undermines God's plan, and man and woman choose to listen to the serpent's instructions rather than those of God.

By failing to exercise their dominion over the serpent, they destroy the trusting harmony God desires within the garden. By betraying God, man and woman are sent forth from the dwelling God prepared for them. Their God-given dominion over the creatures of the earth turns to domination. God's authority is overturned, and harmony begins to revert to the chaos that existed before God formed the world. As the stories of the early chapters of Genesis reveal, the hallmark of sinful humanity becomes violence toward other creatures, both human and animal, and toward God's good creation.

This account in Genesis 3 focuses on the human condition: our desire for happiness and the reality of pain, sin, and death. The storytellers of Israel's wisdom tradition saw how the world is deeply wounded and wondered how human suffering is compatible with belief in a powerful and loving God. With colorful language and the symbols of the garden, the author paints a picture of God's desire for our happiness, yet also of God's desire to create us free, capable of personally choosing God's will for our lives. The human will turned against God's plan, and the result is the suffering and death that comes from sin. The storyteller shows us how it has been *from the beginning* by painting a story of life *in the beginning*.

The symbolic tree, whose forbidden fruit the couple eats, represents the temptation to be autonomous and to live apart from God's reign. Human beings are alive and free to enjoy creation as long as they live out their freedom under God's rule and will for human life. The temptation they face through the serpent is to become a law unto themselves, to walk according to their own path rather than the way of their Creator.

The result of this human choice for autonomy apart from God's way is the destruction of the harmony that God placed within creation. The human relationship with God is distorted. From walking comfortably with God in the garden, man and woman now hide from God's presence in fear and shame. The relationship of man and woman to each other is damaged. They become morbidly self-conscious, quickly covering their nakedness and blaming one another.

Yet, God's purposes are not defeated. Although an uncertain and perilous world faces the couple, God does not abandon them. They will still bear the divine image in the world. Although God punishes by cursing the serpent and putting enmity between the offspring of the serpent and that of the woman, God also offers hope by promising that the offspring of the woman will strike and crush the head of the serpent (Gen 3:15). That is, a descendant of Eve will destroy the powers of evil that the man and woman have unleashed through their disobedience.

Some of the essential truths taught by this account of Adam and Eve are these:

- Human beings are created by God with the ability to choose or reject God's will.

- The root cause of human suffering is sin, the human choice to disobey God.

- Sin disrupts human relationships and brings about shame and blame.

- Suffering is not a punishment inflicted by God, but a consequence of sin.

- Human beings suffer on account of our own sin and the sin of others.

- God doesn't abandon the human race but promises them a future in which to hope.

### The Effect of Sin in the World

The stories of Genesis 3–11 show how the effects of sin multiply and destroy human relationships with God, with other people, and with the created world. After the sin, Adam hides from God; he blames Eve, and he is expelled from the harmony of the garden and made to work for food with hard labor. When Eve gives birth to Cain and Abel, rivalry grows between them. Out of jealousy, Cain murders his brother Abel and must wander alone upon the earth. The family that God desires to be a place of support and companionship becomes a breeding ground for envy, resentment, rage, and vengeance.

Accounts of family rivalry lead up to the story of Noah and the catastrophic flood. Sin has spread throughout the whole earth, and violence and corruption have so filled the world that God regrets making human beings on the earth. In God's desire to remake the world, he saves Noah and his family as well as a remnant of every species upon the earth. God manifests his commitment to creation despite the destructive effects of human beings in the world. Following the flood, God establishes a covenant with every living creature with the rainbow as its sign (Gen 9:8-17).

The final story of sin's expansion is the account of the tower of Babel. Even though the growth of cities and cultural progress can demonstrate human achievement, it is doomed to failure when it demonstrates human autonomy apart from God. The huge tower becomes the symbol of humans' arrogance because of their attempts to go it alone in defiance of the Creator (Gen 11:4). God condemns the human pride that has inspired it and judges the people by confusing their language and scattering them abroad.

These stories describe tendencies that move deep within every person. Men and women are inclined to act in ways that lead to estrangement and blame each other for it. Siblings tend to fight with one another and grow apart. Human beings think they have the power and wisdom of God, and they suffer in their sinful choices. Men and women are good, yet flawed and fallen. Although God passionately wills life and blessing for his creatures, all of these blessings begin to be destroyed because of sin. The power of death gets increasingly stronger and the world begins to return to the chaos from which it came.

Against the background of these early chapters of Genesis, the rest of the Bible narrates the history of salvation. The remainder of Scripture demonstrates how God desires the world to become a dwelling shared by God, humanity, and the creatures of the earth. God's people must be rescued from the control of sin and receive the royal and priestly dignity that God wishes to bestow upon them. The kingdom of God must be established throughout the earth so that God may dwell with his royal and priestly people.

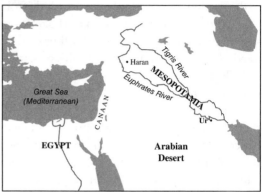

### God Initiates a Saving Plan

Although the stories of Genesis 1–11 show humanity moving away from God, Genesis 12 introduces a different kind of narrative. Against the darkness of human sinfulness, the light of God's saving will begins to shine in the person of Abraham. Beginning with his call, we see Israel looking deep into its own ancient history to recover accounts of its ancestors. These accounts of the origins of Israel go back to the ancient traditions passed on through many generations. The type of writing we see in these narratives can be described as folk history, an ancient history that has been handed down through oral tradition. Though rooted in history, the accounts contain imaginative, symbolic, and legendary material. They have a timeless quality and they teach us powerful lessons about God and faith.

Out of all the scattered nations of the earth, God chooses one family. God called Abraham and Sarah to leave their homeland and go to a new, unknown land—to leave their former identity and find their identity in God. They migrate from Ur of the Chaldeans (in present-day Iraq), up the Euphrates river valley, to Haran in Mesopotamia (a city near the present border of Turkey and Syria). Then, they travel with their whole household to the land of Canaan, which would become the land of Israel many centuries later.

The opening verses of Abraham's call (Gen 12:1-3) preview the covenant God will make with him in the form of three promises. First, God will give Abraham a new land, a land to which God is leading him. Second, God will give Abraham numerous descendants—too many to count—who will form a great nation. And third, God assures Abraham that through him "all the families of the earth will find blessing."

In other words, God doesn't call Abraham just for his own sake, or for his own family, or even for the future people of Israel. Rather, God calls Abraham and enters into covenant with him so that, ultimately, all the people of the world will be blessed. The stories of Abraham demonstrate how God begins to fulfill these promises; the remainder of the Torah shows their partial fulfillment; and the rest of the Bible shows how God fulfills those promises completely.

For all later generations, Abraham becomes the father of faith. Asked to leave his autonomy and security—family, tribe, home, country—he travels a long journey to an uncertain destination, following where God leads him. His faith is marked by his constant relationship with God—a faith that consists of belief in God, trust that God will fulfill the promises, and obedience to God's will.

God is at work, through Abraham, to reverse the curses that sin has brought upon the world. God desires to restore his original blessings and purpose to creation. By giving Abraham's descendants the land, by making them the great nation of Israel, and by ultimately restoring God's blessing to the people of all nations, God makes Abraham his first instrument in the divine plan to redeem the world.

God confirms the covenant with Abraham through sacrificial rituals and concrete signs. The sign of the covenant with Abraham is circumcision, a visible and permanent mark of God's relationship with this people who come from Abraham's loins. After many long years of trusting, God reaffirms the covenant, telling Abraham and Sarah that they will have a son whom they will name Isaac. Sarah's barren womb gives way to God's promise. Although both Abraham and Sarah laugh aloud at the suggestion that they will have a son in their elderly condition, God has the last laugh. God says to Abraham, "Is anything too marvelous for the LORD to do?" (Gen 18:14). When their son is born, they name him Isaac, which means "laughter."

Finally, Abraham's faith is most challenged when God tells him to take his son Isaac and offer him in sacrifice on Mount Moriah. In this unbearable test, Abraham reluctantly but trustingly journeys to put his only beloved son to death. While Isaac carries the wood of the sacrifice, he asks his father, "Where is the sheep for the burnt offering?" And Abraham answered, "God will provide the sheep for the burnt offering" (Gen 22.7-8). At the last moment, God stays his hand. Abraham has demonstrated his faith in the fullest way.

Following this scene, God reaffirms the promises of the covenant: "In your descendants all the nations of the earth will find blessing" (Gen 22:18). This final promise to Abraham frames the narrative of his obedient life, from its early beginning at Abraham's call to its final, climactic end. Later revelation states that Mount Moriah is the temple mount in Jerusalem. Here, in later history, the priests of the temple will make morning and evening sacrificial offerings, a divine sign that God will provide universal blessing for all people. Here, at the place God desires to establish as a house of prayer for all the nations, God desires a final sacrifice, an offering for the sin of all humanity.

## Patriarchs and Matriarchs of God's People

Many centuries after the life of Abraham and Sarah, God spoke through Isaiah the prophet and called God's people to trust in a troubled time: "Look to Abraham, your father, / and to Sarah, who gave you birth; / though he was but one when I called him, / I blessed him and made him many" (Isa 51:2). God calls future generations to imitate the example of Israel's first patriarch and matriarch because the promises God made to them are being fulfilled in every age.

The accounts of Genesis 25–35 narrate the stories of the descendants of Abraham and Sarah. We see that God's promises are reaffirmed to their son and grandson, so that God comes to be referred to as "the God of Abraham, Isaac, and Jacob."

But these stories are filled not only with promises confirmed, but also with bitter family relationships. The one who inherits the promises is not Abraham's first son, Ishmael, born of Sarah's slave girl Hagar, but Isaac, conceived in Sarah's old age by the saving will of God. When Isaac marries Rebekah, they have twin sons. Esau is the first born, then Jacob follows from the womb, gripping Esau's heel and prefiguring a life of conflict between the two sons.

As the boys mature, Jacob uses his cleverness to claim the inheritance that is due to Esau. With the help of his mother, he outwits his father Isaac and his brother Esau to obtain the birthright and become the heir of the covenant promises. Over and over Israel's stories demonstrate that God's promises cannot be merited or taken for granted. They do not belong by right to the natural or most obvious successor; rather, they are the free gift of God.

The feuding between Jacob and Esau plays itself out in a variety of ways as Jacob flees for his life because of Esau's desire to kill him. On his journey, God meets with Jacob through a dream at Bethel. While sleeping, Jacob dreams of a stairway stretching between earth and heaven, with angels traveling up and down on it. God stands beside Jacob, identifies himself, and reaffirms to Jacob the promises made to the family of Abraham.

> I am the LORD, the God of Abraham your father and the God of Isaac; the land on which you are lying I will give to you and your descendants. Your descendants will be like the dust of the earth, and through them you will spread to the west and the east, to the north and the south. In you and your descendants all the families of the earth will find blessing. I am with you and will protect you wherever you go, and bring you back to this land. I will never leave you until I have done what I promised you. (Gen 28:13-15)

Polygamy was common among the people of the ancient Middle East and the people of Israel were no exception. When Jacob desires to take Rachel as his wife, her father offers to give his daughter in marriage after Jacob has worked for him seven years. Then on the night of the wedding, her father deceives Jacob and switches his older daughter, Leah, in the darkness of the marriage chamber. The next morning, when Jacob discovers that he has been deceived and has consummated the marriage with Leah rather than his beloved Rachel, the girls' father promises he will give Jacob his younger daughter after another seven years of Jacob's service to him. The one who used his clever cunning to obtain his own father's blessing now is deceived by the clever father of his wives.

While Leah gives birth to sons, Rachel bears none. Competing to see which side of the family will have the most children, both women offer their maidservants to their husband to bear more children. This rivalry between wives and sons will bring immeasurable jealous division within the family of Jacob.

When Jacob prepares to return to his own land with his two wives, two maidservants, and eleven children, he learns that his brother Esau is coming to meet him after many years of estrangement. Jacob fears that his brother will take revenge for his deception. But on the night before

their meeting, Jacob encounters a divine visitor who wrestles with him throughout the night. When Jacob asks the stranger for a blessing, God changes Jacob's name to Israel, which means "he who wrestles with God." So Jacob becomes the father of the nation that will be formed from the tribes of his sons, a nation what will certainly wrestle with God throughout its history.

At dawn Esau arrives and runs to his brother, weeping and embracing him. Jacob's happy surprise teaches him to trust in God's designs. He does not need to scheme and deceive to obtain God's blessings. Jacob experiences the divine presence in both the love of God and the love of his brother. Here there is hope that forgiveness and reconciliation can prevail over the homicidal jealousy exemplified in Cain and Abel.

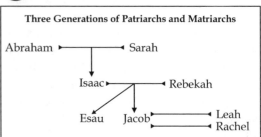

**Three Generations of Patriarchs and Matriarchs**

Abraham ▶──────◀ Sarah

Isaac ▶──────◀ Rebekah

Esau   Jacob ▶──────◀ Leah
                    ◀ Rachel

## The Twelve Sons of Jacob

The children of Rachel and Leah, together with their midwives, number twelve sons: Reuben, Simeon, Levi, Judah, Issachar, Zebulun, Dan, Naphtali, Gad, Asher, Joseph, and Benjamin. These twelve become the patriarchs from whom the twelve tribes of Israel take their descent.

The last section of Genesis, chapters 37–50, contains the stories of Joseph and his relationship to his brothers. Joseph, the first son of Rachel, is Jacob's spoiled and favorite son. His father loves him best and has made him a long ornamented tunic. Joseph's dreams and his ability to interpret them intensify his brothers' jealousy, so they plot to kill him.

Instead they sell him to a band of traders who bring him down to Egypt, but they deceive Jacob into thinking his son has been murdered. They dip Joseph's coat in the blood of a goat, and they tell their father that Joseph has been slain by a wild beast. Again, Jacob reaps what he has sown. Just as Jacob deceived his own father Isaac to obtain his blessing, so now Jacob experiences the betrayal of his own sons' deception.

In Egypt, Joseph becomes a servant to Potiphar, an officer of Pharaoh. Then his fortune changes when he successfully interprets the dreams of Pharaoh and thereby saves Egypt from famine. When Joseph is made a favorite minister of Pharaoh, famine in Canaan brings his brothers to seek help in Egypt. Joseph is now in a position to invite his father and brothers to come down to Egypt to live and escape the famine. Joseph's reunion with his brothers is an emotional event and their father Jacob dies a happy man because he is reunited with his son Joseph.

The account of Joseph reads like a novel that is hard to put down. It is a story of injury and forgiveness, of estrangement and reconciliation. We see the development of Joseph from a selfish and alienated youth to a mature and selfless leader fully reconciled with his family. Through his generosity and willingness to forgive, Joseph upholds the unity of Israel's family and prevents their extinction. Throughout these accounts, the providential hand of God guides the fate of the family of Jacob–Israel as God brings good out of evil and turns disaster into triumph over and over again.

## Moses Called to Be God's Instrument of Liberation

The whole book of Genesis is a preview for the experiences told in the book of Exodus. Most nations can point to a decisive event that constitutes the beginning of their histories. For Israel that event is the exodus. This event gave birth to Israel as a people, as a nation, and as a religion.

The book can be described as epic history. It does not use detailed historical records, but it recounts the oral history remembered by the people of Israel through the ages. It exalts the power of God in the founding events of their life as a people. At its core it is historical, but its focus is on God—the One who cares for his chosen people and passionately desires their freedom.

As Exodus begins, we realize that the seventy members of Jacob's family who went to Egypt have increased abundantly over many generations.

> Now Joseph and all his brothers and that whole generation died. But the Israelites were fruitful and prolific. They multiplied and became so very numerous that the land was filled with them.
> Then a new king, who knew nothing of Joseph, rose to power in Egypt. (Exod 1:6-8)

The first chapters of Exodus are an account of misery and oppression. The new pharaoh fears the numbers of the Israelites, so he subjects them to brutal slave labor and initiates a cruel policy of killing all newborn male Israelites. After a wondrous infancy narrative, showing how the initiative and courage of women rescue Moses and lead him to be raised in the court of Pharaoh, the book recounts how Moses is called to rescue his people.

The call of Moses, like the call of Abraham, marks the beginning of a new stage of God's saving plan. While shepherding sheep in the wilderness, Moses comes to the mountain of God. There he has an astonishing encounter with God, who speaks to him from a burning bush. Telling Moses to take off his sandals because the place and the encounter is holy, God identifies himself to Moses as the God of his ancestors.

> I am the God of your father, he continued, the God of Abraham, the God of Isaac, and the God of Jacob. Moses hid his face, for he was afraid to look at God.
> But the Lord said: I have witnessed the affliction of my people in Egypt and have heard

their cry against their taskmasters, so I know well what they are suffering. Therefore I have come down to rescue them from the power of the Egyptians and lead them up from that land into a good and spacious land, a land flowing with milk and honey, the country of the Canaanites, the Hittites, the Amorites, the Perizzites, the Girgashites, the Hivites and the Jebusites. Now indeed the outcry of the Israelites has reached me, and I have seen how the Egyptians are oppressing them. Now, go! I am sending you to Pharaoh to bring my people, the Israelites, out of Egypt. (Exod 3:6-10)

God initiates the events of the exodus as God sees the wretched state of the people and hears them as they cry out for help. God is determined to rescue them from their oppression. But the exodus event is not just liberation from slavery; it includes the gift of freedom to live in a land of blessings and abundance. The fertile and spacious land of God's promises is the ultimate goal of Israel's redemption. Now God is sending Moses to Pharaoh to be the instrument of Israel's deliverance.

The response of Moses expresses humility and reluctance. When he asks for the divine name so that he can identify God to his people, God responds with the distinctive name by which God will be known throughout the Scriptures. God says, "I am who I am. This is what you are to say to the Israelites: I AM has sent me to you" (Exod 3:14). The divine name, YHWH, is generally written in English versions of the Bible as "LORD." The root verb conveys the idea of dynamic presence. The name conveys this idea of God's active presence in the life of Israel. God will be known through what God does, through the effect God has in the life of the chosen people. The whole of salvation history is God's expression of the divine name.

Moses uses every excuse he can muster to escape his call, yet God reassures him: "I will be with you." Then the presence of God, bringing good from evil, bringing freedom from oppression, is demonstrated in two basic stories of deliverance: first, the plagues in Egypt and Passover (Exod 7–11), and second, the crossing of the sea (Exod 13–15) .

## God Frees the Israelites from Slavery

The obstacle to the Israelites' liberation is Pharaoh, who is regarded by the Egyptians as divine and holding absolute power. The exodus is described as a conflict between the LORD, the God of freedom and life, and Pharaoh, the god of oppression and death. Both assert a claim over the faithfulness and service of the Hebrews. The exodus events express the defeat of the powers of slavery that Pharaoh represents, and they express the liberation of God's people from all that prevents them from becoming the people they were chosen to be.

Through a series of ten plagues, Pharaoh is confronted with the fact that the LORD is God. The LORD's enslaved people are rescued from their oppression on the night of Passover. As the tenth and final plague comes upon the Egyptians, the families of the Israelites are instructed to sacrifice a lamb and to apply its blood to the lintel and the doorposts of their homes. This sacrificial blood prevents death from entering their houses and becomes the doorway through which the families of God will enter into their freedom.

Defeated and desperate, Pharaoh at last lets the Israelites go. But he makes one last attempt to restrain the Israelites and orders his armies to pursue them as they flee Egypt. The Israelites then arrive at the sea, with the Egyptians in hot pursuit. At God's command, Moses stretches out his hand over the sea and the waters are divided, allowing the Israelites to pass through the sea for their final escape to freedom. With the waters divided like a wall to their right and left, the Israelites pass through on dry land just before the break of dawn.

This passage of Israel through the sea is remembered as the primary event of salvation for Israel, expressing in a single event the whole narrative of transition from bondage to freedom. For the ancient Israelites, the sea represents the forces of destruction, chaos, and death. The passage through the waters, from the darkness into the dawn, is an image of birthing, the transition through the birth canal. Israel is God's firstborn, and the exodus is described by later writers as the moment of Israel's birth.

The song of Moses in Exodus 15 celebrates God's magnificent rescue at the sea and describes this liberation as the way God will be continually manifested. God is the one who is repeatedly conquering all those forces opposed to freedom and abundant life: crushing injustice, overcoming domination, and vanquishing oppression. The newborn Israelites praise their God of freedom and life and celebrate God's divine victory over all the forces of oppression and death. The song links Israel's "coming out" of bondage to the people's "coming into" the land.

One of the most important descriptions of God in the Old Testament is "I am the LORD your God, who brought you out of the land of Egypt, out of the house of slavery" (Exod 20:2; Deut 5:6). The liberation of God's people from bondage and their establishment as a people was the decisive event of God's self-revelation to Israel. This passage from bondage and death to freedom and life became the paradigm for describing all of God's future actions of deliverance.

The people of Israel learned to reflect on all the events of their national history in light of the primary event of the exodus. The Israelites expressed their faith in God by reciting the saving deeds they experienced throughout their history, beginning with the exodus and narrating their history with ever-new hope. Because God had heard the people's cries in the past, they could be certain that God would continue to rescue and save them. In every age, Israel knew that its future would take shape according to the same patterns with which its past had been formed.

Over and over again throughout the story of Scripture, people find themselves imprisoned, locked in captivity. And God, with power and compassion, brings them to deliverance and abundant life. This bondage takes many forms and many names in Scripture: slavery, imprisonment, oppression, grief, doubt, sin, death, alienation, and despair. Likewise, the passage to freedom takes many forms and names: rescue, deliverance, ransom, release, passover, redemption, and salvation. This deliverance that God offers is both physical and spiritual, both temporal and eternal.

---

Now that the people of God have passed through the waters, the history of Israel as a nation has begun. Israel was born out of the waters, brought by God out of the waters and into life. Now that Israel is born, God leads her through a period of childhood and adolescence, before she reaches adulthood in the Promised Land. These are the topics we will explore as we complete our survey of the Pentateuch.

## ISRAEL'S FOUNDATIONAL COVENANT

After Israel is given birth through the waters, the formative period of Israel's young life is spent in the wilderness. Here the Israelites learn how to relate to God, how to trust in God's presence, how to worship God, and how to live as a people specially chosen by God. In the wilderness the Israelites begin to leave behind the mentality of slavery and embrace the freedom of serving the LORD, the God who acts on their behalf.

The Torah is inspired through the leadership of Moses. Since it narrates his own death and includes material that was written long after the days of Moses, he is not the "author," in the modern sense of writing the whole work himself, but he is the *author-ity* behind the whole Pentateuch. His obedience to God, his mighty deeds, his mediation for Israel, gives the Pentateuch its lasting form and the core of its ongoing tradition.

The five books of the Pentateuch are focused on Mount Sinai, which is at the heart of the Torah. Genesis and the first eighteen chapters of Exodus lead up to the mountain. In Exodus 19–40, the whole book of Leviticus, and Numbers 1–10, Israel is at Mount Sinai. Then the remainder of Numbers and the book of Deuteronomy show Israel moving from Sinai toward the Promised Land.

**The Pentateuch Focuses on Mount Sinai**

| | |
|---|---|
| Genesis 1–50<br>Exodus 1–18 | Movement toward Mount Sinai |
| Exodus 19–40<br>Leviticus 1–27<br>Numbers 1–10 | Israel is gathered at Mount Sinai |
| Numbers 11–36<br>Deuteronomy 1–34 | Israel moves from Mount Sinai toward the Promised Land |

## Guided to the Mountain of God

After describing the captivity of the Israelites and their liberation through the sea in the first fifteen chapters of Exodus, the following chapters narrate their journey from the sea to the mountain. Along the way, they experience God's saving power in numerous ways. God's guiding, protective presence with the Israelites along the journey is seen in the column of cloud that leads them during the day and column of fire during the night. God's provident, nurturing presence is demonstrated by God's feeding the Israelites with manna and quail and giving them water to drink from the rock.

After three months of desert travel, the Israelites reach the mountain of God, the same area where Moses first encountered the LORD. But now God is not just calling one man for a specific mission; God is calling an entire people to be his own. God is revealed this time not in a burning bush but in an awesome display of thunder, lightning, fire, smoke, and clouds. Israel experiences God as powerful and near.

Through speaking with Moses on the mountain, God reminds the Israelites of what he has done for them. God says that he has brought them out of Egypt like an eagle carrying its tired young on its wings. The deeply relational nature of God's saving activity is expressed in God's words to Israel, "I . . . brought you to myself" (Exod 19:4). Israel is utterly dependent on God's gracious acts for its survival, but God's desire is to have a people with whom he shares a personal relationship.

God calls Israel for a special purpose. God says, "You will be my treasured possession among all peoples" (Exod 19:5). And further, "You will be to me a kingdom of priests, a holy nation" (Exod 19:6). God is seeking to restore the divine image that had been disfigured by human sin. God is beginning to raise up a people who will be royal rulers and priests, through whom all the nations of the earth will be blessed. As a royal priesthood among the nations, Israel is called to be a mediator between the LORD and the other nations and to be a model for other nations of what it means to be in covenant with God. So being chosen by God is not just a special privilege; it is a means of serving God, reflecting the divine image in the world and demonstrating for other nations what living under God's reign looks like.

## Forming the Covenant with God

At Mount Sinai God enters into covenant with Israel, a bond modeled on the relationship of family. The LORD will be the God of Israel and Israel will be the people of God. In covenant, they belong to God, and that family bond implies a relationship that expresses itself in changed behavior.

As an expression of this relationship, God speaks the Ten Commandments, literally "the ten words," to Moses. These form the core of the covenant law. The first three commandments deal with Israel's exclusive worship and relationship with God. The remaining commands deal with the obligations of the Israelites toward one another. These ten are the seed from which all of Israel's legal tradition grows.

Israel's understanding of these commandments is intimately related to their covenant with God. The law, those things that Israel must do as an expression of this bond with God, is a response to what God has already done for Israel. So, obeying the Torah is not another form of slavery. It is rather a loving response to the compassionate care that God has already demonstrated for Israel.

God commanded Pharaoh, "Let my people go to serve me" (Exod 9:1). Israel realized that slavery under Pharaoh led to bondage and death, but servitude under Yhwh leads to freedom and life. Thus obedience to the law of God was Israel's means of expressing their new family relationship with God and the freedom associated with being bonded to God.

The additional legislation found within the Sinai covenant expresses the fact that these texts are the work of many generations of living in the covenant. The Covenant Code—laws regarding slaves, personal injury, property damage, loans, care for the poor, pilgrimage, and the like—sets out in greater detail Israel's obligations: first, to worship God rightly, and second, to deal justly with one another. All aspects of life as a nation come within the scope of God's reign over Israel. How God's people treat one another will forever be a manifestation of how genuinely they worship the Lord. A people who has been rescued from bondage and oppression must never become oppressors in their relationships to the neglected and the powerless in their midst.

Israel's Torah expresses a level of social awareness unmatched in the ancient world. Reading the lists of laws and liturgical regulations throughout the Pentateuch reminds us of the commitment our ancestors made to right living and dedicated worship. Even though many of the social laws and rules of worship no longer apply literally today, they can inspire us to give our very best to God, both in worship and in relationship with God's people. Like Israel, we must try to understand God's commandments not as a constraint that makes life difficult, but as keys to living the fullness of life for which we were made.

Israel confirms their covenant with God at Mount Sinai and seals their bond in a sacrificial liturgy. A covenant requires two willing partners. In Exodus 24, we see that Moses recites all the words and ordinances of the Lord and writes them down. God does not coerce, but invites Israel into a covenant that will make them his people. God's people voice the words of their acceptance, saying, "All that the Lord has said, we will hear and do" (v. 7).

Next, Moses builds an altar and sets up twelve sacred stones, representing the fact that each of the twelve tribes (descendants of Jacob's twelve sons) are entering into this covenant with God. The young men then offer burnt offerings and communion sacrifices in which blood is poured out. This "blood of the covenant" is splashed both on the altar, representing God, and on the people. To share the same blood is to share the same life, to be joined in a family bond.

After this sacrificial rite, Moses and the elders of the people go up the mountain and are given an extraordinary experience: "They saw God, and they ate and drank" (Exod 24:11). They eat and drink the communion sacrifice, an expression of a shared life and family bond with God. The Lord has promised to dwell with his people, and here we see that promise on its way to being fulfilled in an intimate way.

Following the covenant ceremony, the remainder of Israel's history is basically a narration of how faithfully (or unfaithfully) Israel lives up to its call given at Mount Sinai. Israel will be a kingdom of priests and a holy nation to the degree that they adhere to their bond with God as stipulated in the covenant. If they choose to live in the presence of their God and live in obedience under God's reign, then they will live a full and rich life in which the peoples of the world will want to share.

### Building the Ark of the Covenant and the Tabernacle

Although the communion sacrifice experienced by Moses and the elders with God is a transitory event, God desires to dwell among his covenanted people in a permanent way. So the final chapters of Exodus describe God's detailed instructions for building the tabernacle, a tent structure that would, two centuries later, develop into the design for the temple in Jerusalem. This tabernacle in the wilderness will be a portable sanctuary, God's personal residence among the Israelites, as they continue their journey.

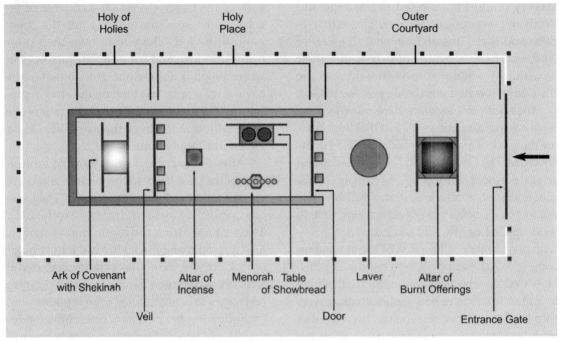

| Holy of Holies | Holy Place | Outer Courtyard |
|---|---|---|

Ark of Covenant with Shekinah · Altar of Incense · Menorah · Table of Showbread · Laver · Altar of Burnt Offerings

Veil · Door · Entrance Gate

The focal point of God's traveling presence amid the people is the ark of the covenant. This wooden chest, plated inside and outside with pure gold, is designed to contain the visible reminders of God's covenant with Israel. The top of the ark is a cover made of pure gold with two golden cherubim at each end, their wings sheltering the cover. There, between the cherubim and above the cover, the invisible God promises to abide among the people.

The other structures for the tabernacle include a golden altar for incense offerings, a golden menorah (the seven-branched lampstand), and a display table with plates containing loaves of bread and pitchers and bowls for wine offerings. Each of these are designed for worship in the divine presence, and each is designed with two golden poles mounted on their sides to that they may be carried along the way.

God instructs that the ark be placed in the holy of holies and that it be separated from these other objects by a purple-scarlet veil. A similar curtain is to be hung at the entrance of the tab-

ernacle. In the courtyard outside the sanctuary, God describes the construction of a large bronze basin filled with water for the washing of the priests and a bronze altar on which burnt sacrifices are offered. Rites for the consecration of priests, the design of priestly vestments, and formulas for anointing oils and incense complete God's instructions for worship at the tabernacle.

No longer are God's people forced to build for the pharaoh; now they willingly donate their talent and treasure to build God's dwelling in their midst. These last chapters of Exodus, detailing the nature and shape of God's portable residence, emphasize that Israel's journey moves from Egyptian slavery to divine service, the worship of the LORD.

But after Moses receives God's instructions for the tabernacle and its construction, Exodus narrates a great rebellion by the people that threatens the covenant itself. While waiting for Moses to descend the mountain, the Israelites become impatient and make for themselves a golden calf. Comparable to the defiance of Adam and Eve in the garden-temple, the people try to replace what God is already providing them. Rather than depend on their unseen and holy LORD, they quickly construct a visible object to replace the divine presence, violating the first of all the commandments. Only the appeal of Moses to God averts the disastrous consequences of a broken covenant. As Moses bows to the ground and begs God's pardon for the wickedness of the people, God passes before Moses on the mountaintop and proclaims:

> "The LORD, the LORD, a God gracious and merciful, slow to anger and abounding in love and fidelity, continuing his love for a thousand generations, and forgiving wickedness, rebellion, and sin; yet not declaring the guilty guiltless, but bringing punishment for their parents' wickedness on children and children's children to the third and fourth generation!" (Exod 34:6-7)

In the face of the people's shameful betrayal, Moses discovers the depth of God's merciful love. The Israelites receive God's forgiveness, yet they are also warned of the inevitable consequences of sin. These treasured words will give hope to rebellious Israelites throughout their history. It will help them understand the consequences of their infidelity, but will enable them to trust that God will always be their God. So, with this understanding of God, the people of Israel construct the tabernacle according to God's directions.

The tabernacle and its liturgy perpetuate God's saving presence in the midst of the people. The liturgical legislation received and enacted at Mount Sinai and the completion of the tabernacle and its liturgical furnishings serve as a kind of portable mountain of God. The once-and-for-all experience of forming the covenant on Sinai is made present again and again as the liturgies of the sanctuary are enacted by the people bound to God in covenant.

The book of Exodus ends as the glory of the LORD fills the tabernacle and God comes to dwell with his people. Freed from Egypt, they are now liberated to desire the LORD. Abounding in love and fidelity for the Israelites, God leads them along their journey.

## The Quest for Holiness

Leviticus, the third book of the Pentateuch, is a collection of covenant legislation regarding worship and the priesthood. Because God has come to dwell with the Israelites, they must become and remain a holy people, a people set apart for God. They must live in a way that reflects the holiness and closeness of God among them. God says, "I, the LORD, am your God. You shall make and keep yourselves holy, because I am holy" (Lev 11:44). "Be holy, for I, the LORD, your God, am holy" (19:2).

Holiness has both a positive and a negative aspect. It is an attachment to God, a way of living that gives honor to God and that recognizes the sacredness of others. Holiness is also a separation from whatever is unholy, impure, unclean, or sinful. Everything dedicated to God—the place of worship, the priests, and the feasts—were set aside from ordinary life and consecrated.

The first part of the book, Leviticus 1–7, describes the rituals for different kinds of sacrifices and offerings. It includes directions for burnt offerings (holocausts), grain offerings, communion sacrifices, purification offerings, and reparation offerings. Israel's sacrifices express gratitude for God's gifts by offering a portion of them back to God. They also demonstrate a recognition of sinfulness and a desire to be restored to a right relationship with God.

The second section, Leviticus 8–10, describes the ordination ritual for Aaron, the brother of Moses, and the sons of Aaron. Since Aaron is from the tribe of Levi, he and his descendants are set apart to be the priests for Israel. Although all the people of God are called to holiness, the priests are further set apart to be the facilitators of the holiness of all. As such, they serve as mediators between God and God's people by leading worship and directing the Israelites in the rituals that structure their lives.

The third part, Leviticus 11–16, is the code of laws regarding legal purity. The foundation of many of these laws remains obscure, but so many of them are related to a deep respect for blood and sexuality. Israel knows that life is a holy mystery with its source in God and that life is intimately connected with blood and sexuality. The loss of any bodily fluids represents in some way a loss of life and so renders one unclean. Often the state of being clean or unclean, pure or impure, is not related to moral choices, but is rather a ritual reality concerned with one's condition for coming into contact with God in worship.

The final section, Leviticus 17–26, is the collection of holiness laws. These regulations concern all aspects of Israel's existence as a holy people whose life is oriented toward the worship of God. In addition to moral laws, Israel has its calendar of feasts to help it recognize the holiness of time. Every week, the Sabbath must be observed. Every year, Israel celebrates the feasts of Passover (Pesach), Pentecost (Shavuot), New Year (Rosh Hashanah), Day of Atonement (Yom Kippur), and Tabernacles (Succoth). Then every seventh year, the Sabbatical Year, provides for a time of rest even for the fields, and every seventh Sabbatical year (every fifty years) brings the Jubilee year, a time of reconciliation and renewal for all of Israel.

All of the legislation of Leviticus is intended to order Israel's life with God. It deals with the reality of an all-holy God living in the midst of a less-than-holy people. It teaches them that God is the source of all life and holiness. All that relates to sin and death is kept apart from the presence of God. God alone has the power to completely conquer sin and death, a promise that God will make throughout the history of his people in the land.

### From the Mountain to the Promised Land

The book of Numbers takes its name from the census or numbering of the people that begins the book. This fourth book of the Torah tells the story of Israel's journey from Mount Sinai, through the wilderness, and finally to the plains of Moab, just outside the Promised Land.

The first ten chapters of Numbers takes place at Mount Sinai, where the people of Israel have been encamped since their encounter with God on the mountain. While Leviticus details the organization of Israel's worship, these pages of Numbers itemize the organization of Israel's community. A census is taken of the men in each tribe who are able to serve in the army, as this group of former slaves becomes a well-ordered force ready for military conquest of the Promised Land.

The tribe of Levi, the priests, is exempted from military service, but their duties are described as central to the life of Israel. Their responsibilities are centered on the ark of the covenant and the tabernacle, the dwelling of God in the midst of the people of Israel. As the final preparations are made to continue the journey, God gives to Aaron and his sons the priestly blessing upon Israel, with its threefold invocation of God's holy name.

> The LORD bless you and keep you!
> The LORD let his face shine upon you, and be gracious to you!
> The LORD look upon you kindly and give you peace! (Num 6:24-26)

As the Israelites set out from Mount Sinai, the narrative takes up again where Exodus left off. The LORD who bore his people on eagle's wings must now teach them how to fly. As they journey through the wilderness, they are led by the guiding presence of God manifested in a column of cloud by day and a column of fire by night. But despite having God in their midst, soon the Israelites begin to complain about the hardships of desert travel.

God's people continually face two temptations along the way. The first is the lure of stopping and settling in place. Although God gives them periodic places of rest along the journey, they are forbidden to settle down for too long. God continually called them from the securities of the present into the unknown risks of the future. The second enticement is turning back to Egypt. The past looks attractive because at least it was secure and predictable. The Israelites were challenged to remember the past, but only in order to live better in the future, not to avoid the future.

The lessons that Israel learns in its wilderness narrative are lasting and recurrent in every age of their covenanted life with God. For later generations who hear these accounts, they serve as both warning and encouragement along the way. Getting Israel out of Egypt is much easier than getting Egypt out of the hearts of God's people. God tests and challenges them along the journey in order to extract their slave attitude and victim mentality, teaching them to trust and filling them with the divine spirit of liberty and the fullness of life.

The worst crisis on the journey comes after Moses has sent a team of scouts to spy out the land of Canaan to which the Israelites are traveling. The scouts report that the land is indeed fertile and fruitful. They carry back a cluster of grapes so large that it requires two men to carry it on a pole between them, and they declare that it is a land flowing with milk and honey. However, they also report that the people of the land are strong and their cities are fortified. The scouts state that they felt like mere grasshoppers in comparison to these people.

The report generates fear among the people, a dread that surmounts the people's trust in God. The Israelites begin to weep and despair of ever reaching their destination. They see only their temporal situation: they are just runaway slaves and cannot hope to accomplish what God is calling them to do. Complaining bitterly they question God's motives, and rebelling against God, they decide to choose a new leader to lead them back to Egypt. This plan marks a rejection of their covenant with God. Once again, only Moses's pleading with God prevents their destruction.

But God declares that none of this faithless generation will enter the land. As a result, the Israelites are made to wander in the wilderness for forty years. Throughout the Bible, the number forty, whether it be forty days or forty years, is a time of testing and preparation for what God is going to do next. The entire generation that was numbered in the census that began the book of Numbers will perish in the wilderness, while their children, the next generation, will one day enter the land God has promised them.

As the long journey continues, the murmurings and rebellion of the Israelites continually

threaten their covenant. They must learn to trust their future to God and to take on a whole new approach to life. The desert period is a time of probation, a time to adjust their attitude of slavery, overcome their fears, and take on a new set of values. God wants them to change their victim mentality and take on the values and lifestyle of a holy nation, God's special possession.

Traditional route of the Exodus
Alternate routes of the Exodus

## The Final Testament of Moses

The final book of the Pentateuch is Deuteronomy. Its setting is the Plains of Moab across the Jordan River, with the Israelites encamped and on the verge of entering the Promised Land. Moses will not enter the land with them, but will die here. Most of the book takes the form of several eloquent speeches given by Moses to the people on the eve of his death. The book is a restatement, explanation, and further development of much of the Pentateuch. By reminding the Israelites of their past and preparing them for the future, he urges them to be faithful to the covenant.

In his first speech (Deut 1–4), Moses reviews the events of the past forty years, from Mount Sinai to the present moment. He tells the new generation of the important lessons learned from the experiences of their parents' generation. This interpersonal union that God has formed with them demands an exclusive worship of the LORD. Israel's constant temptation throughout history will be the worship of other gods and idols. The God who brought Israel out of slavery is the one God.

> This is why you must now acknowledge and fix in your heart, that the LORD is God in the heavens above and on earth below, and that there is no other. And you must keep his statues and commandments which I command you today, that you and your children after you may prosper, and that you may have long life on the land which the LORD, your God, is giving you forever. (Deut 4:39-40)

The future well-being of God's people in the land will depend on their loving and serving God from the heart.

The second address (Deut 5–28) is a restatement and expansion of God's commandments with applications for their future life in the land. Moses reminds the Israelites that the Ten Commandments and all the decrees are rooted in their relationship with God. Following in the way of the covenant is the way to love God with your whole being. The *Shema* forms their daily prayer.

> Hear, O Israel! The LORD is our God, the LORD alone! Therefore, you shall love the LORD, your God, with your whole heart, and with all your whole being, and with your whole strength. Take to heart these words which I command you today. Keep repeating them to your children. Recite them when you are at home and when you are away, when you lie down and when you get up. Bind them on your arm as a sign and let them be as a pendant on your forehead. Write them on the doorposts of your houses and on your gates. (Deut 6:4-9)

The purpose of this book and indeed the whole Torah of Israel is to make the Israelites know how much God loves them and how much God wants them to return that love. God's love for Israel is demonstrated by liberating them from slavery, guiding them through the wilderness, and bringing them into the Promised Land.

Israel's love for God is shown through an active obedience that involves their whole life and is motivated by wholehearted love.

Moses, who knows the challenges that God's people will face as they enter the land, is passionately urging them to remain faithful to the covenant, to the loving and exclusive relationship that God has established with them. Moses knows that if the people of Israel continually repeat these words and allow these words to form their lives, teaching their children to do the same, then they will remain faithfully committed to their God. The covenant should shape their thoughts and actions every day of their lives. If they see these words of instruction when they come and go from their homes, they will remember God's covenant and experience the blessings of a faithful life.

The detailed legislation recounted in Moses's address brings this vision of loving God with one's whole self down to the particular instances of daily life. Living under God's reign has implications for the whole life of the people in the land. Its obligations are both individual and communal—personal, social, spiritual, and political.

In addressing the new generation, Moses urges them to "remember." By remembering, God's people form identity. They become a part of all that God has done in the past. Every generation of Israel must pass on the tradition to their children. They must remember continually, visually, and tangibly, by binding the words of the Torah on their foreheads and on their arms, and upon the door and gates of their dwellings.

By remembering, the past becomes real in the present, and life can be lived more faithfully and genuinely. Each generation is able to share fully in the formative events of Israel. The moment that is most important for the book of Deuteronomy is not the past; it is "this day." The critical time for every person is "today."

> The LORD, our God, made a covenant with us at Horeb; not with our ancestors did he make this covenant, but with us, all of us who are alive here this day. (Deut 5:2-3)

This day the LORD, your God, is commanding you to observe these statutes and ordinances. Be careful, then, to observe them with all your whole heart and with your whole being. Today you have accepted the LORD's agreement: he will be your God, and you will walk in his ways, observe his statutes, commandments, and ordinances, and obey his voice. And today the LORD has accepted your agreement: you will be a people specially his own, as he promised you, you will keep all his commandments, and he will set you high in praise and renown and glory above all nations he has made, and you will be a people holy to the LORD, your God, as he promised. (Deut 26:16-19)

The final address of Moses before his death (Deut 29–33) presents the Israelites with the choice that will determine their future. If they obey the Torah, loving God and walking in God's ways, they will have life and prosperity. If, however, they refuse to listen to God's word and turn to serve other gods, they will have death and doom.

I have set before you life and death, the blessing and the curse. Choose life, then, that you and your descendants may live, by loving the LORD, your God, obeying his voice, and holding fast to him. For that will mean life for you, a long life to live on the land which the LORD swore to your ancestors, to Abraham, Isaac, and Jacob, to give to them. (Deut 30:19-20)

Lastly, after appointing Joshua as his successor, Moses goes up to Mount Nebo, across the Jordan River from the Promised Land. He looks at the land from afar, and he knows that the new generation will live in the land. Then Moses dies and is buried on the mountain. The book concludes, "Since then no prophet has arisen in Israel like Moses" (Deut 34:10). He was the leader of the people, a mediator before God, a wonderworker, teacher, and Israel's greatest prophet. The Torah, given to Israel through Moses, would form the foundation of Israel's life through the centuries.

---

The final editors of the Pentateuch bring together many narratives and traditions from Israel's early history to give us an account of where the Israelites have come from, who they are, and to what they are destined. Genesis shows us Israel's origins; Exodus shows us Israel's birth as a people; Leviticus describes the holy nature of Israel; Numbers describes the organization of Israel; and Deuteronomy shows us the spirit of Israel. The dynamism of these biblical stories always points toward the future.

The promises made by God will be fulfilled only when the blessings of God are extended to the whole of humanity. The God of the Torah is the one who overcomes chaos, death, slavery, and injustice. The LORD is the one who offers freedom and life, who brings his chosen ones into an experience of intimacy with him so that through them all the nations of the earth may be blessed.

The Torah is both narrative and legislation, both story and ethics. The more God's people understand who God is, the more they will know who they are. By hearing and remembering the story, God's people will know how to live. Just as God creates life out of chaos, God's people are to be life-givers and care for life. Just as God frees from slavery and oppression, God's people are to seek justice and liberate others. Just as God is faithful to the covenant, God's people are to be faithful to that relationship of intimate love.

## EXPLORING LESSON ONE

1. The stories found at the beginning of Scripture are stories of spiritual, religious truth rather than historic, scientific fact. After reading about the stories found in Genesis 1–11, what are some of the central truths about God and human beings that are taught here?

_____

_____

_____

_____

_____

2. In the covenant with Abraham, God promises land, numerous descendants, and the assurance that through Abraham, "all the families of the earth will find blessing." Many centuries later, the Gospels of Matthew and Luke trace Jesus' genealogy back to Abraham (Matt 1:1-2 and Luke 3:34). What connection can you make here? How is Jesus the fulfillment of God's promise to Abraham about "all the families of the earth"?

_____

_____

_____

_____

_____

3. The story of Joseph and his jealous brothers (Gen 37) develops into an account of Joseph's rise to favor in the house of Pharaoh and his reunion with his family in Egypt (Gen 42–47). When has God done something unexpected in your life, leading to an improvement or a reunion?

_____

_____

_____

_____

_____

4. What name does God give when Moses asks God to identify his divine name (Exod 3:13-14), and what does this name convey? How is this name usually written in English versions of the Bible?

_____

_____

_____

_____

5. What is the primary event of salvation for the Israelites? What does this event tell them about their God?

_____

_____

_____

_____

_____

6. Exodus 6:2-8 can be read as a kind of summary of much of the Pentateuch (also known as the Torah). Summarize the promises God makes to his people in these verses from Exodus.

_____

_____

_____

_____

_____

7. a) Read Exodus 16, which tells the story of the LORD feeding his people with manna in the desert. How does this story illustrate God's relationship with his people?

_____

_____

_____

b) How can we apply this story to our lives as Christians? How has God nourished the church? How has God nourished you?

_____

_____

_____

8. How would you describe the covenant relationship between God and Israel? How did Israel experience and live the covenant? (In other words, was the covenant a burden for Israel? Were the laws considered restrictive?)

_____

_____

_____

_____

_____

9. a) What is the biblical understanding of "holiness" (Lev 11:44; 19:2)? How did Israel live this holiness in concrete ways?

_____

_____

_____

   b) How are you being invited to live "holiness" in a biblical sense?

_____

_____

_____

10. What were the two main temptations the Israelites faced as they travelled through the desert toward the Promised Land? Do you face either of these temptations in your life?

_____

_____

_____

_____

_____

_____

11. This lesson ends with the following insight: "The more God's people understand who God is, the more they will know who they are." What have the Israelites learned about God? What does this tell them (and us) about how they (and we) are to live?

_____

_____

_____

_____

_____

_____

**CLOSING PRAYER**

*Prayer*

The L<small>ORD</small> bless you and keep you!
The L<small>ORD</small> let his face shine upon you, and be
   gracious to you!
The L<small>ORD</small> look upon you kindly and give
   you peace!   (Num 6:24-26)

O God, we ask this priestly blessing of Israel upon all
your people, and especially upon those who gather to
share in the blessings of your word. May our faces shine
with your light and graciousness, and may we bring
your kindness and peace to those most in need in our
world. Today we pray especially for . . .

## LESSON TWO

## The Historical Books

Begin your personal study and group discussion with a simple and sincere prayer such as:

*Prayer*

*Loving God, you liberated your people and led them to the Promised Land. Liberate our minds and hearts as we study your word, that we may live joyfully as your faithful people.*

Read pages 38–55, Lesson Two.

Respond to the questions on pages 56–58, Exploring Lesson Two.

The Closing Prayer on page 58 is for your personal use and may be used at the end of group discussion.

## FROM CONQUEST TO KINGDOM

The historical writings of the Bible continue the history of the Israelites, beginning with their entry into the land. These books do not attempt to give a detailed and documented presentation of each moment in Israel's history. Rather, they offer God's viewpoint of Israel's history, recounting how the Israelites both follow God's covenant and rebel against God's will through the centuries. The historical books narrate both the workings of God in Israel's history and Israel's response, positive and negative, to God's work.

The books of Joshua, Judges, 1 and 2 Samuel, and 1 and 2 Kings are sometimes called the Deuteronomic history. They cover over 600 years of history, beginning with the death of Moses to the destruction of Jerusalem in 587 BC. Together these books demonstrate the results of that fundamental option offered at the end of Deuteronomy—the choice between life and death, the blessing and the curse. When Israel chooses life and follows the covenant, the blessings promised to Abraham, Isaac, and Jacob follow. But when Israel chooses death and turns away from the covenant with God, destruction and doom follow.

### Overlooking the Holy Land

At the end of the book of Deuteronomy, Moses stands atop Mount Nebo, looking over into the land promised to Israel's ancestors. Canaan is a narrow strip of land along the eastern shore of the Mediterranean Sea, forming the only link between the two ancient centers of civilization in the Middle East—Egypt to the southwest and Mesopotamia to the northeast.

Through the land, from north to south, flows the Jordan River. It originates in the mountains of Lebanon, flows into the Sea of Galilee, then falls into the Dead Sea, nearly 400 meters below sea level. The country is a combination of rocky hill country and lush, fertile plains.

To a people accustomed to the desert, it is, as described earlier in Exodus, "a land flowing with milk and honey." This designation refers to the agricultural bounty of the land and God's nourishment of his people there. Milk refers to the dairy products that result from raising goats and sheep; honey refers to the syrup derived from dates. Moses describes the seven species, the special agricultural products of the land: wheat, barley, grapes, figs, pomegranates, olives, and dates. He then urges the Israelites to always give thanks to God for these gifts.

For the Lord, your God, is bringing you into a good country, a land with streams of water, with springs and fountains welling up in the hills and valleys, a land of wheat and barley, of vines and fig trees and pomegranates, of olive trees and of honey, a land where you will always have bread and where you will lack for nothing, a land whose stones contain iron and in whose hills you can mine copper. But when you have eaten and are satisfied, you must bless the LORD, your God, for the good land he has given you. (Deut 8:7-10)

## Entering into the Land of God's Promise

The book of Joshua is named after the hero of Israel's period of conquest. Joshua succeeds Moses as leader of the Israelites and leads them in the struggle for possession of the land of Canaan. God says to Joshua, "As I was with Moses, I will be with you: I will not leave you nor forsake you" (Josh 1:5). Although the conquest of the land involves fighting battles, the narratives emphasize Israel's dependence on the LORD for their success. As the fulfillment of promises made to their ancestors, the land is God's gift.

The crossing over the Jordan River into the Promised Land is presented as a liturgical procession. Entering the land from the east, the people are led by the priests, carrying the portable ark of the covenant with its golden poles for transport. When the feet of those carrying the ark touch the water, the river stops flowing so that the people may cross over into the land. Just as Moses led God's people across the sea, Joshua leads the next generation across the river into the next stage of their new life.

Joshua chooses a man from each of the twelve tribes and commands each one to take a stone from the riverbed. These are set up just inside the land as a memorial of God's promises fulfilled for the twelve sons of Jacob. Here the men of the new generation of Israelites are circumcised, and here the people celebrate their first Passover in the new land.

The first conquest, the siege of Jericho, is recounted not as a military campaign but rather as a liturgical event. The priests carry the ark of the covenant and blow ram's horns (*shofarim*) as they process around the walls of Jericho. For six days the priests and troops march around the city, then on the seventh day they encircle the city seven times, and with the sound of horns and the shout of the people, the walls of Jericho crumble, as the Israelites take the city and put to the sword all of its living creatures.

The purpose of this literary style is to demonstrate to every generation that God is faithful to the covenant in providing a homeland for the Israelites. Events that took place perhaps over many decades are condensed into a short period of time. The Deuteronomic author does not offer military details but desires to demonstrate how all the events of seizing the land happen according to the covenant.

After Joshua and his army conquer Jericho, they then go on to conquer Ai, Bethel, and Gibeon. A rapid sweep of southern Canaan is followed by the conquest of northern Canaan. After this victorious invasion, the author summarizes the work of Joshua: "Thus Joshua took the whole land, just as the LORD had said to Moses, Joshua gave it to Israel as their heritage, apportioning it among the tribes. And the land had rest from war" (Josh 11:23).

Following Joshua's victories and the division of the land among the tribes of Israel, the end of the book describes Joshua's final farewell to the people at the end of his life and his solemn renewal of the covenant. The ceremony begins as Joshua proclaims all the great deeds that God has done on behalf of Israel, from the call of Abraham to the conquest of the land. Then he urges the people to commit themselves to the service of the LORD, rather than the gods of the Canaanites. Leading by example, Joshua brings the people to make a decision.

"Now, therefore, fear the LORD and serve him completely and sincerely. Cast out the gods your ancestors served beyond the River and in Egypt, and serve the LORD. If it is displeasing to you to serve the LORD, choose today whom you will serve, the gods your ancestors served beyond the River or the gods of the Amorites in whose country you are dwelling.

As for me and my household, we will serve the LORD." (Jos 24:14-15)

After hearing Joshua's recounting of God's faithfulness to Israel, the people answer him, "Far be it from us to forsake the LORD to serve other gods" (v. 16). As they promise Joshua, "We will serve the LORD, our God, and will listen to his voice" (v. 24), he solemnly reaffirms their covenant with God that day at Shechem. Their future in the land that has been given to them will depend on how they choose to live after Joshua's death, on how they love and obey their God.

## Sin, Violence, and Destruction

The violence of Israel's conquest of the land often shocks modern readers of these accounts. Likewise, God's commands to either drive out or put to death the Canaanite inhabitants of the land causes readers to question whether this is the same God they worship. Undoubtedly this period of history was brutal and bloody, and the biblical authors refuse to censor that reality. Yet, the point of view from which these narratives were written, demonstrating Israel's fidelity and infidelity to the covenant, may help explain some of the reasons for recounting the destruction of the former inhabitants of the land.

A detailed history of these times would probably indicate a gradual settlement and incorporation of the Israelites into the land. It seems that the various Canaanite peoples were revolting against Egyptian control of the land. The Israelites were one of several other peoples seeking to claim their stake in the land during this tumultuous period. With this in mind, the military victories may not have been as ruthless and decisive as they are described in the Bible.

Keep in mind that the biblical accounts describe the Israelite understanding of God's will centuries after the events. The battles are described as liturgical events with decisive outcomes in order to emphasize the fulfillment of God's promises to give the land to Israel. The enemies in these accounts represent threats to the covenant. The Canaanite worship of many gods and goddesses, involvement in fertility rituals, and even child sacrifice express the depravity of these people in opposition to genuine worship of the LORD. The complete destruction of these people in these military accounts conveys the importance of wiping out all vestiges of these practices from the Promised Land.

These Canaanites represent for Israel, centuries after the historical conquest, the corrupting and weakening effects of sin. When a community has reached a certain degree of corruption, it is due for destruction because sin itself calls down the just punishment of death. Remaining in sin is to remain alienated from God and on the path to ruin. These Canaanites demonstrate for Israel what turning from God and disobedience to the covenant can also mean for themselves. So the doom of the peoples of Canaan serves as a warning for Israelites tempted to follow other gods and disregard God's statutes for establishing justice in the land.

Surely there were battles and skirmishes during Israel's conquest of the land, but perhaps not the merciless destruction described in these books. Historical evidence and archaeology indicate that the primary shift in the land of Canaan was a gradual one, from political allegiance to Egypt and religious adherence to pagan practices, to the social, cultural, and religious practices stipulated by the covenant statutes and faithfulness to the LORD alone.

## Israel's Tribal Life under the Judges

The book of Judges covers a period of Israel's history between the death of Joshua and the beginnings of Israel's monarchy. It is a rugged, violent, frontier period for the Israelites. What is described in the book of Joshua as a quick sweep of the land is described in the book of Judges as a gradual occupation of the land which is limited and not at all conclusive.

The book describes Israel's transformation from a seminomadic people of the desert to a settled people dependent on agriculture for their livelihood. In religious terms, this transformation involves coming to understand that the God who was revealed to Israel in the wilderness and traveled with Israel along the journey is also the God who will be with the people in their settled life in the land. Israel's adoption of many of the agricultural methods of the Canaanites tempts the Israelites to also adopt features of the fertility religion of the Canaanites. These rituals promise fertility for the land and thus economic success. So time and time again, during this period, Israel falls into idolatry.

During the period of the judges Israel consists of a loose joining of twelve separate tribes, each living in its own area, without any central political or legal authority. Their only bond is the covenant with God, symbolized by the ark of the covenant, located now at Shiloh in the central hill country (see map at the beginning of this chapter). The ark links the tribes now settling in the land with their ancestors who gathered in covenant with God at Sinai. While these separate tribes enjoyed their own autonomy, they would gather at certain times to celebrate religious festivals.

The book of Judges is named for the stories of twelve judges that fill its pages. These judges are not primarily people who make legal decisions but rather military leaders raised up by God in time of need to save the Israelites from destruction. These judges do not lead the whole nation, but single tribes or small groups of tribes against their enemies—the Canaanites and the Philistines.

The stories of Deborah, Gideon, Jephthah, and others are colorful tales that grew up around these heroes of Israel's frontier period. The Deuteronomic writer demonstrates a cyclical pattern that recurs in the account of each judge. First, Israel falls into sin; then, Israel is punished for sin; then Israel repents, and God delivers Israel. But Israel is a slow learner and falls back into sin and repeats the pattern again and again.

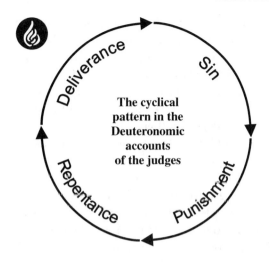

The cyclical pattern in the Deuteronomic accounts of the judges

Deliverance — Sin — Punishment — Repentance

The writer remembers Israel's history from the perspective of obedience or disobedience to their covenant with God. The sin of the Israelites is usually idolatry, worshipping the gods of Canaan. The Israelites are delivered punishment through an invasion by an enemy. In distress, God's people recognize their sin and call out to God for mercy. Then, God delivers them by raising up a judge who rescues them from their oppressor. The cycle runs its course and all is fine again until the Israelites forget the lesson. Then they slide back into idolatry and the whole cycle repeats itself. But this pattern is not just an endless circle. As the sin continues to worsen, the cycle becomes rather a downward spiral into disaster for the Israelites.

Israel's downward spiral can be seen in the descending character of the judges. The earliest judges, like Deborah, are faithful and just, but the later judges become increasingly morally compromised. The last judges seem to be more villains than heroes.

The account of Samson, the final narrative of Judges, serves as a mirror of Israel's behavior. Samson is a Nazirite, one who has taken a vow of separation and holiness. He defeats the Philistines with many amazing feats of strength, yet he continually falls for Philistine women. When he marries Delilah the Philistine, she coaxes Samson into revealing that the secret of his strength is his uncut hair, a symbol of his fidelity to his nazirite consecration. So,

Delilah cuts his hair in his sleep, and when he awakens, his strength is gone. The Philistines gouge out his eyes and throw him into prison.

Samson means "sun" and Delilah means "night." The storyteller is showing how the Israelite sun is darkened by the Philistine night. Israel, strengthened by the covenant, is weakened by yielding to idolatry. After losing its strength, Israel becomes blind by doing what is evil in the eyes of God.

As the story ends, the Philistines are holding a temple feast celebrating the power of their god over the God of Israel. They bring in Samson for some entertainment, but by now his hair has grown back and his strength has been restored. Samson takes his revenge against the Philistines by pulling down the columns of their temple so that the structure collapses, killing the Philistines and himself. Like Samson, Israel has been consecrated to God yet continually falls into the seduction of pagan gods. Samson's tragic fate makes us wonder to what disaster God's people will need to be reduced before they realize the implications of their call to be a holy nation.

The book of Judges ends with these words: "In those days there was no king in Israel; everyone did what was right in their own sight" (21:25). Blindness to the covenant destroys Israel's character and leads to doom. The frustrations and defeats of God's people during this period prove the inadequacy of the temporary institution of the judges and prepared the way for a more centralized rule in Israel.

## Clamoring for a King over Israel

The books of 1 and 2 Samuel are about the institution of Israel's monarchy and its effects on the community of God's people. The clamor for a king arises during the period of the judges when the last of the judges—Samson, Eli, and Samuel—suffer defeat at the hands of the Philistines. These Philistines are newcomers to the land, well-armed and aggressive, determined to dominate the other inhabitants of the land. A great urgency ensues when the ark of the covenant is captured in battle and the most important Israelite center, the shrine-city of Shiloh, is destroyed by the Philistines.

The books take their name from Samuel, who is a priest, prophet, and the final judge of Israel. He is instrumental in Israel's transition from the period of the judges to the monarchy. Although Samuel is the last of the judges, even more significantly he is the first of a long line of prophets who will be both advisers and critics of Israel's kings.

Samuel is a transitional figure for two reasons. First, in him the age of the judges gives way to the age of the prophets. From then on, the prophets will be instruments of God's judgment by confronting and challenging Israel's rulers in their worship, their beliefs, and their faithfulness to the Torah entrusted to Israel. And second, but more important for Israel's history, Samuel is a transitional figure because he ushers in the age of Israel's monarchy.

The editor of 1 Samuel includes two conflicting viewpoints in the book. One views the monarchy as ordained by God for the survival of the people. The other views the monarchy as a mistake because a human king is an affront to the LORD, who is their true king. After their defeat by the Philistines, many among God's people want Israel to have a king like the other great nations. A king will unify the tribes, establish a powerful army, and lead them to military success. But Samuel argues that Israel is not like the other nations. Israel already has a king, and that king is the LORD. Samuel also explains that a king will make unbearable demands upon the people, exact heavy taxes, and conscript their sons into military service. He describes the high price that Israel will pay for its monarchy.

> Samuel delivered the message of the LORD in full to those who were asking him for a king. He told them: "The governance of the king who will rule you will be as follows: He will take your sons and assign them to his chariots and horses, and they will run before his chariot. He will appoint from among them his commanders of thousands and of hundreds. He will make them do his plowing and har-

vesting and produce his weapons of war and chariotry. He will use your daughters as perfumers, cooks, and bakers. He will take your best fields, vineyards, and olive groves, and give them to his servants. He will tithe your crops and grape harvests to give to his officials and his servants. He will take your male and female slaves, as well as your best oxen and donkeys, and use them to do his work. He will also tithe your flocks. As for you, you will become his slaves. On that day you will cry out because of the king whom you have chosen, but the LORD will not answer you on that day." (1 Sam 8:10-18)

But the people refuse to listen to Samuel's warnings and continue to insist on a king. So God commands Samuel to give way and provide a king for Israel.

God chooses Saul, and Samuel anoints Saul with oil as a sign of God's spirit upon Israel's first king. Samuel's role as prophet and king-maker is to provide regulation for the king, so that his royal authority does not rival the sovereignty of God. The new monarchy must remain compatible with Israel's covenant. The struggle between kingship and prophecy, political aims and covenant obligations, characterizes the ensuing history of God's people until the end of the monarchy and their exile.

## Saul's Unfaithful Rule

At first, Saul gives the people new unity and hope as he leads the nation to military success over the Philistines. But soon, Saul falls from God's favor as his arrogance, rebellion, jealousy, and paranoia lead him to increasing infidelity to the covenant. Finally, Samuel reproaches Saul, withdrawing his support and the divine legitimacy of the king's rule: "Because you have rejected the word of the LORD, / the LORD in turn has rejected you as king" (1 Sam 15:23).

Samuel is told by God to anoint another king. The choice for king belongs to God, not the prophet or the people. God leads Samuel to Bethlehem in order to determine who among the sons of Jesse God will choose. When the six older sons are rejected, Samuel calls for the youngest son, David, who is tending sheep in the fields.

> Jesse had the young man brought to them. He was ruddy, a youth with beautiful eyes, and good looking. The LORD said: There—anoint him, for this is the one! Then Samuel, with the horn of oil in hand, anointed him in the midst of his brothers, and from that day on, the spirit of the LORD rushed upon David. (1 Sam 16:12-13)

David is just a boy when Samuel privately anoints him as Israel's future ruler. David's selection shows again how God chooses the least to carry out the divine plan. As God says to Samuel: "God does not see as a mortal, who sees the appearance. The LORD looks into the heart" (1 Sam 16:7). So while Saul remains as king, David is God's choice to follow him to the throne of Israel.

As David begins to appear on the scene, the character of Saul falls further and further into disgrace. As Saul is tormented with anxiety, he calls for a harpist to soothe his spirit. Little does he realize that the young man from Bethlehem called to the camp to calm the king's mental turmoil will be the one to usurp his throne. Saul soon becomes fond of the young David and makes him his armor-bearer. At first David thrives in the presence of Saul. With daring trust in God, David gains acclaim by defeating Goliath, a giant Philistine sent out to intimidate the Israelites. David then befriends Saul's son Jonathan and marries Michal, one of Saul's daughters.

David wins the admiration of Israel's women for his military success. When they shower him with greater praise than they give to Saul, the king falls into jealous torment and begins to seek David's death. The younger one is forced to flee and become a fugitive. Gathering a band of followers, David prospers under God's blessing and wins a string of military successes. Although David has several opportunities during this period to kill Saul, David refuses to lay a hand on Saul for he is the LORD's anointed.

At the end of forty years, Saul's reign has collapsed. Facing the defeat of his own army at the hands of the Philistines and the death of his son Jonathan, Saul takes his own life by falling on his sword. David, faithful to the king to his death, mourns the death of Saul and Jonathan, his beloved friend. The bleak narrative of Israel's first king points out the dangers of a human monarch for Israel. God wants a leader for Israel who will enhance God's reign over the Israelites and enable them to live up to the calling of their covenant with God.

The Bible reports acts of rubbing, smearing, or pouring oil on a person or an object. Exodus 30:22-33 describes the composition and use of **"anointing oil"** (v. 25) that was used to anoint cultic objects like the tent of meeting and the ark of the covenant, as well as cultic personnel. This special composition was not meant for the ordinary anointing of the body but was confined to liturgical use.

The anointing of a person usually carried special status. Kings, priests, and at least one prophet (Elisha, see 1 Kgs 19:16) were anointed. Samuel's anointing of Saul and David was intended to show that God had chosen each as king. Anointing made the king a sacred person and empowered him to represent the people of Israel in liturgical ceremonies.

The New Testament confesses Jesus as the Messiah, i.e., "the anointed one," though the Old Testament never uses the term to speak of a coming redeemer or savior. Early Jewish literature including the Dead Sea Scrolls occasionally uses this term in connection with divine deliverance that will take place in the future.

## The Royal Reign of David

The book of 2 Samuel covers the reign of David, his early rule over Judah followed by his reign over the united and holy nation of Israel. David is remembered as Israel's ideal king, a man after God's own heart. The personality of David is vividly portrayed in these narratives, and we are able to know him better than any other Old Testament character. He understands that God is Israel's true king and that he himself is bound to God's covenant.

King David brings new vision to Israel. Within a few years he transforms the Israelites from a divided and dispirited conglomeration of tribes into a united nation. He sets up government structures, builds a palace, strengthens Israel's army, sets up trade with foreign nations, and begins Israel's greatest period as a powerful kingdom.

David's reign is marked by several great accomplishments that affect the ongoing development of God's saving plan. First, David captures the city of Jerusalem from the Jebusites, a city strategically located both militarily and politically. David sets up his own government here and it becomes the capital of the united kingdom. Jerusalem becomes known forever as "the city of David." Second, David decisively defeats the Philistines. With the defeat of these and other enemies of Israel, David's kingdom is powerful and his reign is peaceful. And third, David brings the ark of the covenant to Jerusalem, making the city not only the political capital of the nation but also the religious center (2 Sam 5–6).

Jerusalem is the ideal city for the center of Israel's life. As an ancient fortress city, its height makes it easy to defend from enemies. It is also located north of Judah so that it belongs neither to the northern or the southern tribes and serves to unite the tribes of the north with those of the south. David wants to rise above factional disputes and unite the scattered tribes into a single nation.

In moving the ark to Jerusalem, David demonstrates that the monarchy in Israel is not a denial of the kingship of God. Rather, it is God's instrument to promote the holiness of

God's kingdom. Under David, the ark of the covenant is once more housed in a tent in the midst of the people. As God has dwelt with the Israelites in the desert, so now God dwells with the nation of Israel in Jerusalem. As God's anointed one, this ideal king will preserve Israel in covenant. The bond formed with God through Moses in the wilderness will now be maintained through the king.

## God's Covenant with King David

The primary purpose of all the books in the Deuteronomic history is to demonstrate the establishment of the reign of King David. They show how the covenant of God with Israel will be bound up with the family of David and how his reign will be the instrument through which God will work out the ultimate destiny of Israel.

The climactic passage of these books of Samuel expresses David's desire to build a "house" for the LORD. From his royal palace, David laments that he is living in a house of cedar, while the ark of God dwells in a tent. The word for "house" in Hebrew can mean either temple or dynasty. David states that he wants to build a house for God, a temple where God may dwell among the Israelites. But God speaks through David's prophet Nathan, saying that God will instead build a house for David, a dynasty that will last through the ages.

In this passage God establishes a covenant with David, promising David that his "house"— his dynasty and his kingdom—is firmly established forever. Although David's heir will build a temple for God's dwelling, the throne of David will always be firmly established.

> The LORD also declares to you that the LORD will make a house for you: when your days have been completed and you rest with your ancestors, I will raise up your offspring after you, sprung from your loins, and I will establish his kingdom. He it is who shall build a house for my name, and I will establish his royal throne forever. I will be a father to him, and he shall be a son to me. If he does wrong,

> I will reprove him with a human rod and with human punishments; but I will not withdraw my favor from him as I withdrew it from Saul who was before you. Your house and your kingdom are firm forever before me; your throne shall be firmly established forever. In accordance with all these words and this whole vision Nathan spoke to David. (2 Sam 7:11-17)

This oracle of Nathan emphasizes the everlasting quality of God's covenant with David by the threefold repetition of "forever." Even if David or his heirs fall away, God will remain faithful to his people through the house and kingdom of David. The relationship between God and the king descended from David will be like a father and a son. Although God will chasten individual kings who do wrong, he will not withdraw his favor but will remain true to this divine promise.

The covenant made with Abraham establishes the "family of God," the covenant made with Moses establishes the "people of God," and now the covenant with David establishes the "kingdom of God." The Israelites place their future hopes in David. This mortal king, chosen by God and anointed with God's spirit, becomes "the LORD's anointed one" or *messiah*, and this promise of an eternal reign will provide the foundation for Israel's expectation of the coming of its future messiah.

## The Sin of David

As ideal a ruler as David seems, the narrative of his life includes his sin. When David sees the beautiful Bathsheba bathing from the roof of his royal palace, he sends for her. After David sleeps with her and she conceives a child, David's sin begins to multiply.

David attempts a quick cover-up by calling her husband, Uriah, home from battle. David expects that Uriah will sleep with his wife and so assume her child is his own. But Uriah refuses to sleep with his wife as an expression of solidarity with his fellow soldiers away in battle. The nobility of Uriah and the courage of the soldiers contrasts with the luxury and deceit of their king.

David then arranges the death of Uriah by ordering him to be placed on the front lines of battle. With Uriah out of the way, David takes Bathsheba as his wife. Although David repents and confesses his double sin of adultery and murder, the effects of David's original sin continue to spread throughout the kingdom. The child born from the affair dies, and the many sons of David vie for the throne. Before his death, David arranges that his son Solomon be anointed the new king.

As David lies dying, he summons Solomon and urges him to be faithful to the covenant. Recognizing that the kingdom does not depend on military might or political strategy, David instructs his son to walk devotedly in God's ways. The kingship is God's gift and is now enfolded in the covenant of God with Israel. The remaining history of the monarch is interpreted through the conflict between human sin and the unconditional promises of God.

---

As we consider these inspired books of our religious tradition, they seem saturated with deceit, aggression, and conflict. Although we can discern the thread of God's plan to redeem the world in these books of Israel's early history, these writings also form the national history of an ancient people, a history that is filled with war and peace, lust and love, deceit and faithfulness. Set within the whole of Scripture, these founding narratives form an early part of Israel's evolving understanding of God's will. Practices that seem common in early centuries, such as polygamy and destruction of enemies, are challenged in later centuries as Israel comes to understand God's will and plan more fully.

If these books convince us of one thing, it is that human choices often have disastrous results and that people are in need of salvation. Sin can only be overcome through the unmerited intervention of God in human history to restore what is lost. The Deuteronomic history

(Joshua, Judges, 1 and 2 Samuel, and 1 and 2 Kings) seeks to convince us that what is truly important is not victory or defeat in battle. Rather, what is crucial is loving faithfulness in relationship with God. One's connection with God's covenant determines everything else, not only the fate of individual Israelites, but the fate of the kingdom of Israel as well.

Although Israel's monarchy comes through the people's imprudent desires for national security, in time God will transform the earthly monarchy into an image of his own kingdom, a reign that will eventually produce the reign of God's messiah.

## DIVISION, EXILE, AND RESTORATION

For more than four centuries, the Israelites are administered by a monarchical form of government. The early period of the monarchy is a period of great prosperity and power for Israel, yet it also contains the seeds of its own destruction. Despite the glory of the kingdom, many of Samuel's warnings concerning the monarchy begin to play out during the reigns of Israel's kings.

The kings of Israel primarily fulfill three different functions: military, legal, and religious. As the military leader of the nation, the king is responsible for the defense of the land and its people. This involves providing fortifications, drafting an army, furnishing weapons, waging war, creating alliances with neighbors, and establishing international policies and relations.

The king is also responsible for upholding justice in the land. He settles disputes that arise and adjudicates legal cases. The king must promote the well-being of all the people and especially support the rights of the poor, widows, and orphans of the land.

When the king is anointed, he becomes a unique instrument of God and a channel of God's blessings to the nation. Being particularly intimate with God, he is accountable for the religious institutions in the land. He holds authority over the priests and the worship of Israel, and he himself performs priestly functions and offers sacrifice on important occasions.

## The Reign of King Solomon

The book of 1 Kings begins with the rise of King Solomon. The son of David and Bathsheba, Solomon is chosen by his elderly father over several of his older brothers. He consolidates David's kingdom during a long reign and brings Israel to the most powerful and influential stage of its history.

Solomon is most recognized for his wisdom. After Solomon offers an elaborate sacrifice, God responds by appearing to him in a dream and offering him whatever he wishes. Solomon answers by declaring himself inadequate for being the king and requests the gift that will best enable him to rule God's people well.

> Solomon answered: "You have shown great kindness to your servant, David my father, because he walked before you with fidelity, justice, and an upright heart; and you have continued this great kindness toward him today, giving him a son to sit upon his throne. Now, LORD, my God, you have made me, your servant, king to succeed David my father; but I am a mere youth, not knowing at all how to act—I, your servant, among the people you have chosen, a people so vast that it cannot be numbered or counted. Give your servant, therefore, a listening heart to judge your people and to distinguish between good and evil. For who is able to give judgment for this vast people of yours?" (1 Kings 3:6-9)

God is pleased that Solomon asks for the gift of wisdom before all other gifts—before power, prestige, and possessions. Solomon recognizes himself to be a limited and fallible human creature, totally dependent on God. So God gives Solomon wisdom and exceptional understanding and knowledge. The writer says that his wisdom surpasses the wisdom of all the people of the East. People come from all nations to hear and learn from him. Later tradition associates the wisdom writings with Solomon: the Song of Songs, Ecclesiastes, Proverbs, and the book of Wisdom.

In fact, God is so pleased with Solomon's prayer for "a listening heart" that God also grants Solomon riches and glory that would rival those of any other king. At first, Solomon uses the three gifts that God gives him—wisdom, riches, and universal renown—for the benefit of the people he serves. Among his many accomplishments, Solomon develops Israel's structure of government by dividing the kingdom into twelve administrative districts, each of them governed by a prefect. He develops a powerful corps of horsemen and chariots, using chariots for the first time in Israel's battles, and builds fortress cities for arms and supplies throughout the kingdom. In addition, he builds a defensive wall around Jerusalem and constructs a magnificent palace for his royal court. Giving glory to the nation, he establishes Israel as a center for learning and the arts, as well as international trade. Under Solomon, Israel reaches the peak of its expanse, its wealth, and its fame among the nations.

## A Temple for God's Dwelling

King Solomon's most important accomplishment was the construction of the temple in Jerusalem (1 Kgs 6–7). Although King David desired to honor God with a permanent dwelling, this work is carried out by his son. By building this magnificent house of worship, Solomon continues the concentration of Israel's faith traditions that David has begun in the city of Jerusalem.

Solomon uses only the finest materials and spares no expense in the construction of the temple. Inside the walls are covered with cedar and decorated with carvings of flowers, fruits, and palm trees, evoking the garden of Eden. As in the primordial garden, God dwells here with his people in this temple-garden. The temple also evokes Mount Sinai, as the traditions of the exodus are transferred to the mount of the temple. The sanctuary in Jerusalem now becomes the point of contact between heaven and earth.

When the ark of the covenant is brought into the temple, the journey of the Israelites out of captivity seems to be complete. God and Israel are now at rest in the land. When Moses built the tabernacle for God in the wilderness and the cloud settled down upon it, the glory of the LORD filled the tabernacle such that Moses could not even enter it (Exod 40:34-35). Likewise, after the priests install the ark of the covenant in the holy of holies in Jerusalem, a cloud engulfs the temple so that the priests are no longer able to minister there because of the glory of the LORD that fills the sanctuary.

Because of the temple, the Promised Land is now the Holy Land, and the city of Jerusalem is now the holy city. Now the whole people are able to dwell with God at this place where God has chosen to dwell. Israel must now adhere to this one place for worship and there experience its political, social, religious unity.

Many attempts have been made to construct models of this first temple. Like other ancient temples, it is a three-part structure. At the front of the temple is the portico with its altar of sacrifice. The entrance way is marked by two huge bronze columns. Beyond this entrance is the nave or holy place, containing the incense altar, the table of showbread, ten golden lampstands, and other furnishings. Then beyond the nave is the inner sanctuary or holy of holies. Here stand two huge cherubim whose combined wings span the width of the room. Under the wings of the cherubim lies the ark of the covenant.

At the ceremony of dedication, Solomon expresses the tensions inherent in constructing a temple for God's dwelling. He understands that no human structure can enclose the Creator of the universe. "I am who I am" is everywhere yet contained nowhere. Yet, these material structures of worship mediate God's presence with Israel.

> "Is God indeed to dwell on earth? If the heavens and the highest heavens cannot contain you, how much less this house which I have built! Regard kindly the prayer and petition of your servant, LORD, my God, and listen to the cry of supplication which I, your servant, utter before you this day. May your eyes be open night and day toward this house, the place of which you said, My name shall be there; listen to the prayer your servant makes toward this place. Listen to the petition of your servant and of your people Israel which they offer toward this place. Listen, from the place of your enthronement, heaven, listen and forgive." (1 Kgs 8:27-30)

The temple enables the whole people to dwell with God. God is transcendent, yet God is also intimately present with his holy people, in their holy land, in the holy city.

The temple and its worship express Israel's covenant relationship with God. It is the responsibility of the king to maintain the people in holiness. He must walk blamelessly before God, trusting in the LORD, observing the Torah, and honoring the covenant. Because in and through Israel, God has chosen to reveal himself to all the peoples of the earth.

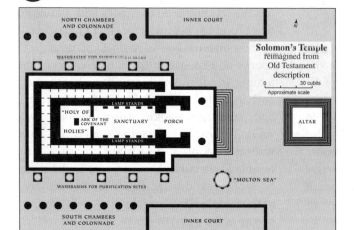

NORTH CHAMBERS AND COLONNADE

INNER COURT

N

**Solomon's Temple**
reimagined from Old Testament description

0        30 cubits
Approximate scale

WASHBASINS FOR PURIFICATION RITES

LAMP STANDS

"HOLY OF HOLIES"   ARK OF THE COVENANT   SANCTUARY   PORCH

LAMP STANDS

ALTAR

WASHBASINS FOR PURIFICATION RITES

"MOLTON SEA"

SOUTH CHAMBERS AND COLONNADE

INNER COURT

### Solomon Sows the Seeds of Division

At the completion of the temple's dedication, God appears again to

Solomon and states which aspects of the covenant are unconditional and which parts depend on the fidelity of Israel's kings.

> The LORD said to him: I have heard the prayer of petition which you offered in my presence. I have consecrated this house which you have built and I set my name there forever; my eyes and my heart shall be there always. As for you, if you walk before me as David your father did, wholeheartedly and uprightly, doing all that I have commanded you, keeping my statutes and ordinances, I will establish your royal throne over Israel forever, as I promised David your father: There shall never be wanting someone from your line on the throne of Israel. But if ever you and your descendants turn from following me, fail to keep my commandments and statutes which I set before you, and proceed to serve other gods and bow down to them, I will cut off Israel from the land I gave them and repudiate the house I have consecrated for my name. Israel shall become a proverb and a byword among all nations, and this house shall become a heap of ruins. (1 Kgs 9:3-8)

Despite the wisdom of Solomon, and in the midst of all the glorious achievements of his reign, the seeds are being sown that will yield a bitter harvest. The statutes of Deuteronomy specify that the man chosen by God to be king over Israel must beware of three things: "He shall not have a great number of horses; nor shall he make his people go back again to Egypt to acquire many horses, for the LORD said to you, Do not go back that way again. Neither shall he have a great number of wives, lest his heart turn away, nor shall he accumulate a vast amount of silver and gold" (Deut 17:16-17).

Weapons, wives, and wealth—these will be the downfall of Solomon and so many kings after him. The untamed drive for power, pleasure, and possessions deny the covenant in which God commands Israel: "I am the LORD your God, who brought you out of the land of Egypt, out of the house of slavery. You shall not have other gods beside me" (Deut 5:6-7).

In order to pay for all his building projects Solomon imposes excessive taxes on the people and drafts many into forced labor. This causes deep resentment among the tribes, especially those in the North who grumble that they are bearing an excessive burden of the extravagance of Solomon's court. In addition, the gulf between the rich and the poor widens. The people complain that the poor live in hovels while Solomon's horses live in stables of ivory.

Solomon's extravagance extends to his huge harem of seven hundred wives and three hundred concubines. His many foreign wives, brought to Israel to create political alliances with other nations, carry with them the religious practices of their own countries and even their own idols. And Solomon does little or nothing to prevent these foreign religious practices and beliefs from influencing the faith of Israel.

The humility, fidelity, and trust required of God's servant, the king, become engulfed by the forces of power, lust, and wealth that rage within the human spirit. Rather than establishing a holy nation and a kingdom of priests, Solomon ends up building a typical kingdom of this world.

## The Kingdom Divided

During Solomon's reign civil unrest begins to surface, and at his death the fragile kingdom cracks. Rehoboam succeeds his father as king and refuses the demands of the northern tribes to ease the taxation and forced labor. He provokes a revolt that will never heal. The northern tribes choose Jeroboam I as king and break away from Judah. The unity that David had established collapses, and from then on the kingdom is divided. The northern ten tribes are thereafter called Israel and the southern kingdom is called Judah.

The political and religious consequences of this schism are enormous. The once-united kingdom is now divided against itself, each part regarding the other as an enemy. Both kingdoms are weaker and far more vulnerable to their enemies. The parallel histories of the northern and southern kingdoms until the destruction of Israel by Assyria are told in 1 Kings 12 through 2 Kings 17.

Jeroboam immediately begins to separate his people from worship in Jerusalem and he establishes religious shrines for sacrifice in Bethel and Dan. Here he sets up golden calves, repeating the sin of the Israelites at Sinai. The weakness caused by division and the idolatry at shrines of worship leads to the gradual decline of the northern kingdom toward disaster.

Assyria is the great empire of the period. After a succession of kings in Israel, Assyrian troops invade the northern kingdom and lay siege to its capital, Samaria, for three years. Israel falls to the armies of Assyria in 721 BC, marking the end of the northern kingdom. Many Israelites are deported to Assyria and people from five foreign populations are brought into the northern kingdom around the city of Samaria. The mixing and intermarriage of the Israelites and these foreigners has led later generations to call these people Samaritans. The Jewish people to this day either ignore or detest the Samaritans, considering them as unfaithful apostates. In John's gospel we will see Jesus accuse the Samaritan woman of having five husbands, an allusion to the five nations who compromised the covenant faith of the people with their own gods and religious practices.

The conquered northern kingdom wonders if God has abandoned the covenant promises to Abraham, Moses, and David. How could God have allowed them to be taken from the land? The narrator makes clear that the people were conquered because the Israelites sinned against the LORD. They venerated other gods and followed the religious practices of other peoples, serving idols and even offering their children in sacrifice.

> The LORD warned Israel and Judah by every prophet and seer: Give up your evil ways and keep my commandments and statutes, in accordance with the entire law which I enjoined on your ancestors and which I sent you by my servants the prophets. But they did not listen. They grew as stiff-necked as their ancestors, who had not believed in the LORD, their God. They rejected his statutes, the covenant he had made with their ancestors, and the warnings he had given them. They followed emptiness

and became empty; they followed the surrounding nations whom the LORD had commanded them not to imitate. (2 Kgs 17:13-15)

## The Fall of Judah

The remaining chapters of 2 Kings tell of the last kings of Judah, the southern kingdom. Judah maintains the succession of kings in the dynasty of David. In relating the lives of each king, the Deuteronomic writer focuses on their fidelity (or infidelity) to the LORD. Unfortunately their general tendency is to follow the terrible example of the north. Most of the kings rule unfaithfully, failing to keep the covenant, thus contributing to the kingdom's decline.

However, two kings of Judah stand out as faithful. King Hezekiah, reigning from 715 to 687 BC, revolts against Assyria and initiates a religious reform. Although Assyria attacks and pillages much of Judah, Jerusalem is miraculously spared and Hezekiah retains his throne. The other faithful king is Josiah, reigning from 640 to 609 BC. He bases his religious reform movement on the book of the covenant, discovered in the temple during his reign. He repudiates Assyrian gods and centralizes the worship of God in Jerusalem. Leading the people of Judah in public repentance, he renews God's covenant with them.

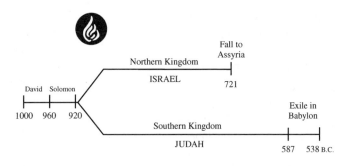

Josiah pleases God through his actions, but it seems to be too little too late. The people's tendency toward apostasy continues into the next generations. The fall of Assyria during Josiah's reign opens the way for the rise of Babylon. Then, after several more unfaithful kings, Babylon invades the southern kingdom. During the reign of King Zedekiah, the armies of Babylon set fire to the temple and the king's palace. In 587 BC Jerusalem is destroyed and all the religious institutions of God's people are in ruin. The great nation established by David and Solomon has died. Many are killed; others flee and go down to Egypt and other places. The king and the leading citizens are all taken into captivity in Babylon.

The deportation to Babylon seems like the end. Jerusalem and its temple are destroyed. Where is God while Babylon triumphs over the people of God? What has come of God's assurances that David's lineage will continue forever? What has happened to God's promises to redeem the nations of the world through the descendants of Abraham?

The seeming end of Israel as a nation does not mark the end of God or of God's promises. Although the Israelites are crushed and defeated, God is still the LORD and the divine purposes endure. Although God has graciously lived in the land with his people, God is not confined to the land.

The double book of Kings ends with a glimpse of hope. The new king of Babylon frees King Jehoiachin of Judah from prison and invites him to eat regularly at his royal table. Perhaps the story of Israel and the lineage of David has in fact not ended.

### The Exile in Babylon

The period of exile in Babylon is a bittersweet time for God's people. It marks a time of painful suffering and longing for what is lost. Yet, through the pain God is purifying the people of Israel to mold them into something new. Those brought to Babylon are many of the intellectual and religious leaders of the people. During the years of exile they seek to keep alive the faith and identity of the Israelites. Many begin to collect the traditions and writings of Israel and edit them into parts of what we know today as the Scriptures of Israel.

The catastrophe of the destruction of Jerusalem and the exile is given expression in the book of Lamentations, a series of laments demonstrating heart-wrenching grief.

How solitary sits the city,
　　once filled with people.
She who was great among the nations
　　is now like a widow.
Once a princess among the provinces,
　　now a toiling slave.
She weeps incessantly in the night,
　　her cheeks damp with tears.
She has no one to comfort her
　　from all her lovers;
Her friends have all betrayed her,
　　and become her enemies.

Judah has gone into exile,
　　after oppression and harsh labor;
She dwells among the nations,
　　yet finds no rest:
All her pursuers overtake her
　　in the narrow straits.

The roads to Zion mourn,
　　empty of pilgrims to her feasts.

All her gateways are desolate,
    her priests groan,
Her young women grieve;
    her lot is bitter.

Her foes have come out on top,
    her enemies are secure;
Because the LORD has afflicted her
    for her many rebellions.
Her children have gone away,
    captive before the foe. (Lam 1:1-5)

With its focus on the LORD, Lamentations also holds out the possibility of regeneration and eventual restoration. Although God's people suffer exile in Babylon, God's presence is far wider than the temple and their city. God is the LORD of the nations and the God of all creation.

Just fifty years after the exile, in 538 BC, the Persians emerge on the world stage and conquer the Babylonians. The Persian king Cyrus gives his conquered people the freedom to maintain their own identity within the empire, and thus he decrees that the people of Israel may return to their own land if they wish and begin their life and worship anew. Many do return, although many do not.

To the Jews, Cyrus seems like a messenger sent from God. The LORD has moved the heart of Cyrus to release the exiles. The book of Ezra recounts the liberating decree:

> The LORD stirred up the spirit of Cyrus king of Persia to issue a proclamation throughout his entire kingdom, both by word of mouth and in writing: "Thus says Cyrus, king of Persia: 'All the kingdoms of the earth the LORD, the God of heaven, has given to me, and he has charged me to build him a house in Jerusalem, which is in Judah. Those among you who belong to any part of his people, may their God be with them! Let them go up to Jerusalem in Judah to build the house of the LORD the God of Israel, that is, the God who is in Jerusalem. Let all those who have survived, in whatever place they may have lived, be assisted by the people of that place with silver, gold, goods, and livestock, together with voluntary offerings for the house of God in Jerusalem.'"

> Then the heads of ancestral houses of Judah and Benjamin and the priests and Levites—everyone, that is, whose spirit had been stirred up by God—prepared to go up to build the house of the LORD in Jerusalem. (Ezra 1:1-5)

Thus, after a generation and more of exile, some of the people of Judah return to the land. The prophets describe this return from captivity in epic dimensions, as a new exodus. But upon their return the people are disappointed and disillusioned. Jerusalem is in ruins, surrounded by hostile neighbors, and the worship of the people who remain has been compromised with many pagan elements. They are now faced with the monumental task of rebuilding the city and its temple.

### The Return and Restoration

The period of history after the exile is known as the restoration, a time of rebuilding the temple and city, reflecting on Israel's identity, and renewing its religious tradition. The two leading figures of this period are Ezra and Nehemiah. They both help the Jewish people become conscious of their calling as God's chosen people, set apart from other nations. Ezra, a priest and scribe, forms the Jewish people into the people of the Torah. Upon arriving in Jerusalem from exile, he reads and explains the holy books. He desires to help the gathered people reclaim the tradition of their ancestors and maintain their identity. Nehemiah helps the Jews reestablish themselves as a nation by rebuilding the walls of Jerusalem, repopulating Jerusalem, forbidding intermarriage with pagans, and restoring observance of the Sabbath.

Much of the history of this period is known from the works of an inspired writer called the Chronicler. The works of this author include the books of 1 and 2 Chronicles, Ezra, and Nehemiah. The work is designed to give an idealized history of Israel with a focus on the dynasty of David and the temple of Jerusalem. Israel's undying hope for a glorious future still focuses on two things: a future anointed one in the line of David and God's dwelling with his people in the temple.

The books of 1 and 2 Chronicles summarize much of the sacred history contained in the Pentateuch and the Deuteronomic history. The Chronicler places special emphasis on David and the kings who descend from David's lineage. The writer also focuses on the construction of the temple and the relationship of Judah's kings to temple worship. It is an idealized narrative in which the sins of David and the weaknesses of his reign are omitted. Israel is shown to be a holy nation, a kingdom of priests, set apart for the worship of God.

The writer takes up the history of the community after the exile in the books of Ezra and Nehemiah. Ezra 1–6 describes the return and resettlement of the first exiles in Judea followed by the rebuilding of the altar and the temple. Ezra 7–10 describes the return of Ezra with a second group of exiles and the reforms of Ezra. Nehemiah 1–7 describes the return of Nehemiah, the rebuilding of Jerusalem's walls, and the census of the people. Nehemiah 8–13 describes the renewal of the covenant and the religious reforms instituted by Ezra and Nehemiah.

When the temple is rebuilt and dedicated in 515 BC, the structure is disappointing to those who remembered or were told of the glorious temple of Solomon. However, most of the Jewish people remain outside their homeland. These Jews living among the nations are called the Diaspora, "the scattered." Their primary challenge is maintaining their distinctive covenant identity and the religious observances that reinforce it. For this purpose, the Jews establish synagogues for Sabbath worship, prayer, and study of the Scriptures. In the midst of an alien culture, the synagogue provides an educational, social, and economic center.

For most Jews, the synagogue cannot entirely replace the temple in Jerusalem. Diaspora Jews continue to revere the temple and hope for its future glory. They go up to Jerusalem for its great pilgrim feasts and continue paying taxes to the temple. They maintain their belief that the one and only God has chosen them to serve him in the temple and to live under the direction of his word. Their own sinful infidelity has kept them from receiving what God has promised, yet they also know that God remains faithful to the divine word given to their ancestors. Although they are being punished for their sin, God will restore Israel to the glory intended for his people. God will complete his saving work through a future redemptive act, and as a priestly kingdom, they will share God's blessings with all the nations in which they are scattered.

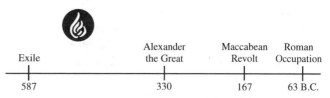

| | Exile | Alexander the Great | Maccabean Revolt | Roman Occupation |
|---|---|---|---|---|
| | 587 | 330 | 167 | 63 B.C. |

## The Occupation by Greeks and Romans

Following the period of the Restoration, the Jews remaining in their homeland live under the domination of one foreign power after another. In about 330 BC the Persian Empire comes to an end with the conquest of Alexander the Great. His rule spreads the Greek language, culture, and religion throughout the Middle East, and Jews throughout this Greek empire feel as though the exile is continuing. Many see this Greek influence, called Hellenism, and the pressure to conform to its culture as a serious threat to their faith and mission.

When Alexander dies without an heir, his empire is divided among his generals, resulting in two dynasties: the Ptolemies in Egypt and the Seleucids. Caught between these two rival powers, Israel, now called Palestine, is first ruled by the Ptolemies (311–198 BC) and then by the Seleucids (198–164 BC). The threat to the Jews comes to a dramatic climax during the reign of the Seleucid king Antiochus IV Epiphanes. He seeks to unify his subjects by imposing Greek culture on them by force. In order to homogenize his empire, the king outlaws Jewish practices such as circumcision,

Sabbath observance, temple sacrifices, and dietary restrictions. The final blow comes as Antiochus sets up a statue of the Greek god Zeus in the temple of Jerusalem and offers a pig in sacrifice, the most unclean animal in Jewish law. Those who refused to worship the god and participate in the sacrifice are mercilessly tortured and killed.

The biblical account of this period is found in the books of 1 and 2 Maccabees. The books narrate how Jewish persecution is met with Jewish revolt under the elderly priest Mattathias and his five sons. When Mattathias is forced to offer sacrifice to a pagan god, he refuses and kills his persecutor. After his brave defiance, he flees to the desert with his sons and forms a band of rebels. When the old priest dies, the movement is taken over by his third son, Judah, who is nicknamed Maccabee, "the hammer," and those loyal to him come to be called Maccabeans.

These Maccabeans win many remarkable battles, and in 164 BC, Judah Maccabee rides into Jerusalem and recaptures the temple. He cleanses the temple of its impurities, removes the images of Greek gods, and rededicates the sanctuary to the LORD. This incredible deliverance of the Jews from their overlords and the dedication of the temple is commemorated each year by the Jews in the feast of Hanukkah.

The book of 1 Maccabees is religious history, narrating the heroic exploits of the five Maccabees fighting for the survival of the Jewish faith and way of life. Although the book does not use the name of God, the book makes clear that it is God's providence that guides their successes. The book of 2 Maccabees comes from the same period, but written by a different author with a different style. It appeals to the emotions and imagination of the readers with an idealistic, edifying, and inspiring account of the events culminating in the rededication of the temple. The work is an important witness to Jewish belief in the resurrection of the just, prayer for the dead, and the intercession of the saints.

The removal of Seleucid rule from the land inaugurates a period of Jewish self-rule under the Hasmoneans. The Maccabean revolt and the eighty years of independence that follow become a defining moment in Jewish history. Since God has acted in this dramatic act of redemption, they believe that God will act again to deliver his people from oppression and to establish the kingdom of God.

But this climactic deliverance does not occur—at least not right away. Rome has been steadily gaining in power since the days of the Greek Empire. Now in 63 BC the Roman general Pompey marches his army into Jerusalem and brings the Jewish homeland into the Roman Empire. The rule of Rome over its subjects is indirect, through cooperative kings and governors. In 37 BC Herod the Great is made king over Palestine, supported by his friend Octavian who becomes Caesar Augustus. The land is ruled by Herod and his descendants, followed by a series of procurators, including Pontius Pilate. The Roman government also appoints the high priest of the temple, assuring a compliant religious system in Jerusalem.

The resentment always felt by the Jewish people against their occupiers now has a new target in Rome, the strongest and most brutal of them all. The Romans crush any sense of Jewish autonomy, forcing their own culture upon their subjects, imposing cruel taxes, and inflicting savage crucifixions upon all who oppose their will. Jewish hatred for Gentiles increases, spilling over to include Roman-appointed tax collectors, temple officials, kings, governors, and all who collaborate with Rome.

First-century Palestine is feverish with both fears and hopes. It maintains its stance as an obstinate province of the empire. Revolutionary movements break out often against the hated Roman overlords, but they are swiftly crushed, ending with mass crucifixions of the would-be rebels, a horrific demonstration of the price to be paid for opposing the empire.

---

As the Israelites' opposition to their foreign oppressors grows, God's people long for the age to come when God will liberate his people from their enemies just as they were delivered from

Egypt and Babylon. When God comes to rule again, he will set things right. Israel will live again in communion with God, who will come again to his temple and dwell among his people.

God's mighty work will be accompanied by the messiah, the anointed king or priest who will be the divine agent of redemption and usher in God's kingdom. Meanwhile, God's people will study the Scriptures, obey the Torah as best they can, celebrate the festivals in their synagogues and occasionally in Jerusalem, and wait in longing for the messiah.

| Hebrews | A name for the Israelite people most often used by strangers or foreigners (see Exod 1:16, 19; 2:6); "Hebrew" also refers to the language of most of the Old Testament. |
|---|---|
| Israelites | Descendants of Jacob, whose other name is Israel (Gen 32:29); the common term for God's people until the Babylonian exile in sixth century B.C. |
| Jews | People of Judah; the common term for the descendants of Jacob during and after the Babylonian exile. The tribe and territory of Judah were all that remained of ancient Israel after the Assyrian deportation of the northern tribes in 722 B.C. |
| Israelis | Citizens of modern Israel. |

## EXPLORING LESSON TWO

1. The book of Joshua describes a sometimes violent conquest of the land of Canaan by the Israelite people. What historical and spiritual factors should we consider as we read these accounts?

_____

_____

_____

_____

2. a) What was the role of the judges among the tribes of Israel?

_____

_____

_____

   b) Describe the cyclical pattern that recurs in the accounts of each judge. What is the typical sin of Israel during this time?

_____

_____

_____

3. How is Samuel a transitional figure in Israel's history?

_____

_____

_____

_____

4. Describe the two conflicting views of the Israelite monarchy found in the books of 1 and 2 Samuel. (See 1 Sam 8:10-22; 10:17-27; 12:13-18 versus 1 Sam 9:15–10:8; 2 Sam 7:8-16.)

_____

_____

_____

_____

5. a) What are David's strengths and weaknesses as a king of Israel?

_____

_____

_____

b) What is God's covenant promise to David?

_____

_____

_____

6 Among King Solomon's many accomplishments was the building of the temple in Jerusalem. What does Solomon's prayer on this occasion express (1 Kgs 8:27-30)? How is God both transcendent and present to his people (then and now)?

_____

_____

_____

_____

7. What three weaknesses prove to be the downfall of King Solomon? How do they demonstrate a lack of fidelity to God?

_____

_____

_____

_____

8. How does the narrator of 2 Kings explain the defeat of both the Northern Kingdom (Israel) and the Southern Kingdom (Judah) despite God's covenant promises to Abraham, Moses, and David?

_____

_____

_____

_____

9. What did the Israelites know about their God that gave them hope even during exile that they would be restored as a nation to their land and temple?

_____

_____

_____

_____

_____

*Lesson Two*

10. How did the oppression of Israel by the Greek and Roman empires lead to an increase in Israel's hope for a messiah, or anointed one?

_____

_____

_____

_____

## CLOSING PRAYER

*Prayer*

*It is God who has saved all his people and has restored to all of them their inheritance, the kingdom, the priesthood, and the sacred rites, as he promised through the law. For we hope in God, that he will soon have mercy on us and gather us together from everywhere under the heavens to his holy place.* (2 Macc 2:17-18a)

God of all peoples, give us the faith of ancient Israel, that we may believe in your presence and your promises. Restore us when we are weak; have mercy on us when we sin; gather us together when we scatter. Hear our prayers today for those most in need of your liberating, restoring presence, especially . . .

# LESSON THREE

## The Writings

Begin your personal study and group discussion with a simple and sincere prayer such as:

*Prayer*

*Loving God, you liberated your people and led them to the Promised Land. Liberate our minds and hearts as we study your word, that we may live joyfully as your faithful people.*

Read pages 60–76, Lesson Three.

Respond to the questions on pages 77–79, Exploring Lesson Three.

The Closing Prayer on page 79 is for your personal use and may be used at the end of group discussion.

## ISRAEL'S SONGS AND STORIES

The Scriptures of Israel are composed of the Pentateuch (*Torah*), the Prophets (*Nevi'im*), and the Writings (*Ketuvim*). This anthology of sacred literature finds its greatest variety in the section of Writings, which includes poetry, songs, prayers, romance, philosophy, and stories.

This assortment of books is remarkable for its humanity, heartfelt expression, and depth of emotion. These writings are less a revelation of God than a response to God's revelation. Each expresses a hard-won commitment to God and the covenant through centuries of trial. In addition to their articulation of rock-solid faith, they dare to voice questions and doubts about God in the midst of danger and suffering.

We first look at the variety of poetic songs in this literature, and then we will glimpse the short stories and novellas that form a part of this literary collection of God's people. A sampling of these writings will demonstrate the variety of literary forms through which divine truth, goodness, and beauty are expressed in the Bible.

### The Psalms of God's People

Songs can be found scattered throughout the Bible. For example, after describing the Israelites' crossing of the sea during their escape from Egypt, the writer of Exodus inserts the Song of Moses and the refrain sung by Miriam (Exod 15). Music and song have been a part of Israel's temple worship from the beginning. String, wind, and percussion instruments accompany both solo and choral voices, often on a grand scale. Song has always been understood in Israel as a fitting response to what God has done for his people.

A collection of 150 songs is contained in the book of Psalms. This compilation is sometimes called the hymnbook of the temple or Israel's prayer book. Perhaps the most important thing to consider about the Psalms is that they are prayers. Their language and purpose differ from most other parts of the Bible as they are intended to express praise, gratitude, grief, and petition to God.

The Psalms are filled with feeling. They contain probably every human emotion possible, from joy, hope, and thanksgiving to anger, frustration, and desperation. Nothing about us can be hidden from God, so the psalms are genuine and honest expressions of feeling arising from the human heart.

These sung poems include hymns for public celebrations in the temple, individual meditations at times of danger or suffering, expressions of awe at God's creation, and much more. Taken together the Psalms offer us a broad impression of the temple, priesthood, and nation, but individually they offer us personal voices expressing peril, doubt, and celebration.

 **David** is the **patron saint of the psalms**. Over half the psalms belong to the Davidic collection. This does not mean that David composed all these works, but rather the superscriptions indicate how these psalms should be prayed in the spirit of David and with his faith. David certainly wrote some of the psalms and is known as a singer and poet (1 Sam 16:14-23; 2 Sam 1:17-27; 1 Chr 29:10-19; 2 Chr 29:30). In addition, he is described as zealous in promoting and beautifying Israel's liturgical prayer (1 Chr 25:1-2; 2 Chr 29:25-27; 35:15; Ezra 3:10). So it is fitting that the whole Psalter is put under his patronage.

## The Psalms as Poetry

Poetry is found throughout the Bible and is exemplified by the Psalms. Poetic language has many characteristics that distinguish it from prose. Words in poetry are chosen for their effect on the imagination, not just for communicating information. For example, personification gives human characteristics to inanimate objects, animals, or ideas. "Let all the trees of the forest rejoice" (Ps 96:12) intensifies the praise given to God in the psalm. Metaphor establishes a correspondence between two phenomena. The language of the psalms is highly metaphorical, keeping the expression vivid and fresh by avoiding abstractness and clichés. For example, in the psalms God is a shepherd, a king, a shield, and a fortress. The clouds are God's chariot and the mountains skip like rams.

Some aspects of Hebrew poetry can be read in the original language, but do not translate well into English. For example, meter and rhythm concern the number of accented syllables in each line. This can be *approximated* when translated, but it rarely matches the meter and rhythm of the original. Onomatopocia is a word that imitates the sound it represents, like sizzle, meow, honk, and boom. These imitative words are also found in Hebrew poetry, but can rarely be translated with the same effect. Alliteration is a poetic device in which a number of words, having the same first consonant sound, occur close together in a series. These closing words to James Joyce's *Dubliners* would not translate effectively into Hebrew: "His soul swooned slowly as he heard the snow falling faintly through the universe and faintly falling, like the descent of their last end, upon all the living and the dead." Likewise, similar alliteration in Hebrew poetry does not translate into English with the same poetic effect.

The most defining characteristic in Hebrew poetry, an aspect that translates fairly well into English, is parallelism. Lines of Hebrew poetry are generally formed in pairs. The second line of a pair repeats, echoes, or balances the thought of the first.

In synonymous parallelism, the second line restates the first in different words. For example, "The heavens declare the glory of God; / the firmament proclaims the works of his hands" (Ps 19:2). "The heavens" finds an echo in "the firmament" or the sky. "The glory of God" partners with "the work of his hands."

In contrasting parallelism, the two lines balance one another or contrast a thought. For example, "For humble people you save; / haughty eyes you bring low" (Ps 18:28). The two lines are parallel, but instead of saying the same thing twice the psalmist expresses the opposite or contrasting idea in the second line.

Comparative parallelism involves a simile or a metaphor. The thought expressed in one line is compared to that of the other, as in "For as the heavens tower over the earth, / so his mercy towers over those who fear him. / As far as the east is from the west, / so far has he removed our sins from us" (Ps 103:11-12). In these two lines of comparative parallelism, the vertical and horizontal dimensions of the cosmos express the height and breadth of God's forgiving mercy.

There are many other types of parallelism found in Hebrew poetry. Sometimes, the parallel lines simply continue the thought of the first line. These are often extended into a third or fourth line. The lines are balanced in form and length, but are not synonymous, contrasting, or comparative parallelism. In modern translations, the psalms are broken down into poetic lines, helping the reader to see the parallel lines of thought that are being expressed.

## Psalms Teaching the Grand Narrative of Israel

The psalms frequently express events from the Torah and the historical books. They teach the people their own story during Israel's liturgical worship by reviewing the major events in the relationship between God and his people. The theme of Israel's sin is often countered with the theme of God's mighty works.

Psalm 105 rehearses the events of Abraham and the patriarchal period.

> He the LORD, is our God
>> whose judgments reach through all the earth.
> He remembers forever his covenant,
>> the word he commanded for a thousand
>>> generations,
> Which he made with Abraham,
>> and swore to Isaac,
> And ratified in a statute for Jacob,
>> an everlasting covenant for Israel:
> "To you I give the land of Canaan,
>> your own allotted inheritance." (Ps 105:7-11)

The psalm continues to recount the story of Joseph sold into slavery, his rule over Egypt, and the entry of Jacob and his sons into Egypt during a famine.

Many psalms recall the events of the exodus and Israel's wandering in the wilderness.

> In the sight of their ancestors God did wonders,
>> in the land of Egypt, the plain of Zoan.
> He split the sea and led them across,
>> making the waters stand like walls.
> He led them with a cloud by day,
>> all night with the light of fire.
> He split rocks in the desert,
>> gave water to drink, abundant as the deeps
>>> of the sea.
> He made streams flow from crags,
>> caused rivers of water to flow down.
>
> But they went on sinning against him,
>> rebelling against the Most High in the desert.
> They tested God in their hearts,
>> demanding the food they craved. (Ps 78:12-18)

This psalm continues to relate God's many signs and wonders in the wilderness in contrast to the ways the Israelites tested God with their demands. Despite God's nourishing them with manna and meat, the people went on sinning. Although they rebelled against God again and again, God compassionately forgave them and redeemed them from their foes.

When the Israelites entered the land, God changed the wilderness to fertile land. God settled his people there and made them flourish with abundance.

> He changed the desert into pools of water,
>> arid land into springs of water,
> And settled the hungry there;
>> they built a city to live in.
> They sowed fields and planted vineyards,
>> brought in an abundant harvest. (Ps 107:35-37)

Psalm 89 extols God's promises to King David. God has made a covenant with David, and God's faithfulness will last from age to age.

> I have chosen David, my servant;
>> with my holy oil I have anointed him.
> My hand will be with him;
>> my arm will make him strong.
> No enemy shall outwit him,
>> nor shall the wicked defeat him.
> I will crush his foes before him,
>> strike down those who hate him.
> My faithfulness and mercy will be with him;
>> through my name his horn will be exalted.
> I will set his hand upon the sea,
>> his right hand upon the rivers.
> He shall cry to me, 'You are my father,
>> my God, the Rock of my salvation!'
> I myself make him the firstborn,
>> Most High over the kings of the earth.
> Forever I will maintain my mercy for him;
>> my covenant with him stands firm.
> I will establish his dynasty forever,
>> his throne as the days of the heavens.
>> (Ps 89:21-30)

The psalm continues by declaring that if the royal descendants of David do not follow the Torah, their deeds will be punished. But God will remain faithful to his promises to David no matter what. God will not violate the covenant and David's dynasty will continue forever, like the sun and the moon, "forever firm in the sky."

Yet, when the monarchy is crushed by Israel's enemies and Jerusalem laid waste, God's people exiled in Babylon continue to long for their homeland.

> By the rivers of Babylon
>   there we sat weeping
>   when we remembered Zion.
> On the poplars in its midst
>   we hung up our harps.
> For there our captors asked us
>   for the words of a song;
> Our tormentors, for joy:
>   "Sing for us a song of Zion!"
> But how could we sing a song of the LORD
>   in a foreign land?
>
> If I forget you, Jerusalem,
>   may my right hand forget.
> May my tongue stick to my palate
>   if I do not remember you,
> If I do not exalt Jerusalem
>   beyond all my delights. (Ps 137:1-6)

The psalmist swears an oath by what is most dear to a musician: the right hand for plucking the lyre and the tongue for singing the psalms.

The psalms leave the readers in the same place as the Pentateuch and the historical books—confident in God's faithfulness to the covenant, yet exiled in foreign lands. As in all the literature of the Old Testament, God's people wonder what God is going to do next, while they trust in God's covenant with Abraham, Moses, and David.

In Psalm 136 the psalmist names deed after deed that God has done for Israel, followed with the refrain, "for his mercy endures forever." All of the historical psalms call God's people to repentance, but also to praise and thanksgiving. They point beyond the mere history of Israel, and they proclaim the LORD who redeems Israel despite its history.

## Types of Prayer in the Psalms

The most common type of psalm is a *prayer of lament*, which cries out to God for help in times of trouble. Death, defeat, illness, guilt,

betrayal—these are all life experiences that the Israelites take to God in prayer. In these prayers they face the situation head on in honest dialogue with God. In the laments we find powerful emotions that sometimes modern readers feel should not be part of prayer—like anger, hatred, complaint, and desire for revenge. But our spiritual ancestors knew one of the foundational principles of modern psychology: pain that cannot be shared is pain that cannot be healed. They knew that we cannot deal with pain by ignoring it, but by acknowledging it and moving through it.

The phrase "my God" is heard over and over again in the lament psalms, underlining the reality that all of these prayers in times of trial are uttered within a conscious and personal relationship with God. Psalm 22 begins with an anguished cry to God, but then develops into an expression of deep trust.

> My God, my God, why have you abandoned
>     me?
>   Why so far from my call for help,
>   from my cries of anguish?
> My God, I call by day, but you do not answer;
>   by night, but I have no relief.
> Yet you are enthroned as the Holy One;
>   you are the glory of Israel.
> In you our fathers trusted;
>   they trusted and you rescued them.
> To you they cried out and they escaped;
>   in you they trusted and were not
>       disappointed. (Ps 22:2-6)

Another type of psalm is a *prayer of praise*. Some of these songs describe who God is and others praise God for his acts. God is the creator of the world and the guardian and protector of Israel. The prayer of praise is well exemplified by Psalm 117, the shortest of all the psalms.

> Praise the LORD, all you nations!
>   Extol him, all you peoples!
> His mercy for us is strong;
>   the faithfulness of the LORD is forever.
> Hallelujah!

Another category is the *psalm of thanksgiving*. This type of song often expresses thanks to God after being delivered from a crisis. This prayer of thanksgiving forms a link between lament and praise. In a time of trouble, the worshiper has been helped or rescued by God. The psalms express amazement at the presence and power of God in a situation that is beyond human abilities. Psalm 30 concludes with a typical expression of thanksgiving.

> You changed my mourning into dancing;
>> you took off my sackcloth
>> and clothed me with gladness.
> So that my glory may praise you
>> and not be silent.
> O LORD, my God,
>> forever will I give you thanks. (Ps 30:12-13)

A related group comprises the *psalms of trust*. The confidence of those who sing this prayer rests in the LORD, the God of the covenant. Because God has been with Israel's ancestors in the past, God can now be trusted to lead the way into a hopeful future. These psalms express a mature confidence, the confidence of those who have experienced trials and failures, but looking back realize that God has been with them. Probably the best known of all these is Psalm 23. God is the good shepherd who leads his people through the dark valley, gives them life-giving waters, and spreads a banquet before them.

The *royal psalms* praise the kings of Israel, the mediators between God and God's people. These psalms extol the rule of David and the line of kings who descend from him. The king is the anointed one of God, the *messiah* in Hebrew, the one honored as the adopted son of God. Psalm 2 proclaims God's decree for his chosen son.

> "I myself have installed my king
>> on Zion, my holy mountain."
> I will proclaim the decree of the LORD,
>> he said to me, "You are my son;
>> today I have begotten you.
> Ask it of me,
>> and I will give you the nations as your
>>> inheritance,
>> and, as your possession, the ends of the
>>> earth." (Ps 2:6-8)

After the exile, when there is no longer a monarchy in Judah, God's people continue to pray these royal psalms in expectation of a future anointed one, the ideal son of David, the Messiah.

A final category of the songs of Israel is the *wisdom psalms*. Through these prayers the people of Israel reflect on the type of life that God desires. They express the singer's desire to know God's will and to follow it in daily life. The book of Psalms begins with a wisdom psalm, describing two ways of life: the way of the just leads to prosperity and the way of the wicked leads to ruin. We recall this same choice given to Israel in Deuteronomy 30, the choice between life and prosperity, death and doom. Like the Pentateuch the psalms urge Israel to choose the way of life.

> Blessed is the man who does not walk
>> in the counsel of the wicked,
> Nor stand in the way of sinners,
>> nor sit in company with scoffers.
> Rather, the law of the LORD is his joy;
>> and on his law he meditates day and night.
> He is like a tree
>> planted near streams of water,
>> that yields its fruit in season;
> Its leaves never wither;
>> whatever he does prospers. (Ps 1:1-3)

While Psalm 1 urges us to meditate on the Scriptures as the means of choosing life, the book of Psalms concludes with a series of songs of praise to God—Psalms 145–150. They express the great joy to be found in choosing the way of God. The book ends with this climactic orchestra of praise to God.

> Hallelujah!
> Praise God in his holy sanctuary;
>> give praise in the mighty dome of heaven.
> Give praise for his mighty deeds,
>> praise him for his great majesty.
> Give praise with blasts upon the horn,
>> praise him with harp and lyre.
> Give praise with tambourines and dance,
>> praise him with strings and pipes.

Give praise with crashing cymbals,
  praise him with sounding cymbals.
Let everything that has breath
  give praise to the LORD!
Hallelujah! (Ps 150)

Not all the psalms fit into neat classifications, but all the psalms can teach us to pray better. They expand our vocabulary and imagery of prayer. They teach us to be totally open and honest before God, helping us break out of any routine or limitations we have placed on our communication with God. We can make these ancient prayers our own, and then allow the psalms to lead us into the prayer that arises from our own hearts. That is why people in every age have turned to the psalms, the prayer book of Israel, as their own book of prayer.

 The **psalms** are the heart of the church's daily prayer in the **Liturgy of the Hours**. The prayer at every prescribed time—Morning Prayer, Daytime Prayer, Evening Prayer, and Night Prayer—as well as the Office of Readings, consists primarily of psalms. The church inherited this practice of using psalms for daily prayer from Judaism and continues it to this day in gratitude for the privilege of praising God with the prayer book of Jesus. Early Christian writers heard every one of these Old Testament prayers as either a prayer of Christ, a prayer to Christ, or a prayer about Christ. Saint Augustine, for example, often points out that even though Christ our head is in heaven, the Body of Christ on earth still cries out in lament as well as praise. Those who pray the Liturgy of the Hours take on the responsibility of giving voice to Christ's members, praying in the name of the whole church and the whole world.

## The Song of Songs

Another book of the Bible is composed exclusively of sung poetry—the Song of Songs. The book is a collection of love poems that describe human romance. Essentially it takes the form of a longing, often passionate dialogue between a man and a woman who love each other. The songs describe sexual attraction and the delights of human love as part of the beauty and goodness of God's creation. Vivid imagery of fruits and flowers, gazelles, fawns, doves, and foxes are all mentioned as part of this pastoral, lyric poetry. The love of the man and the woman are presented within the context of this beautiful, pastoral scene.

The poetry sings of love's joys and passions and its desire for faithfulness.

Set me as a seal upon your heart,
  as a seal upon your arm;
For Love is strong as Death,
  longing is fierce as Sheol.
Its arrows are arrows of fire,
  flames of the divine.
Deep waters cannot quench love,
  nor rivers sweep it away. (Song 8:6-7)

The people of Israel realize that committed, sexual love is a reflection of God's love. This book, which seems to be speaking only of romantic human love, is understood to be sacred writing because the committed love of man and woman is an image of God's love for his people. The songs were understood by Israel as a call to love God, tenderly and passionately.

## The Short Stories of Israel

As in the literature of all people, Israel has its share of short stories. They are some of the favorite literary works of God's people. While they have historical settings and contain some history, their primary purpose is not to give historical information about Israel, but to instruct, console, and entertain.

They read like historical novels—set in a period of Israel's history, but more enjoyable and uplifting than the historical books. The Hebrew Bible classifies most of these stories as Writings, the third category after the Torah and Prophets. In the Christian canon of the Old Testament, they are found scattered in various parts of the Bible. In form they should be classified somewhere between the historical writings and the wisdom literature.

These five books—Ruth, Tobit, Judith, Esther, and Jonah—are some of the most captivating reading in the Bible. Generation after generation has been uplifted and enthralled by them. They are vivid in their setting and details, and their characters are charming and inspiring, with many human traits with which we can easily relate. In the midst of biblical literature filled with tales of men, most of these charming stories present courageous and admirable women who inspire us with their fidelity and their creativity in responding to the covenant.

## The Book of Ruth

The book of Ruth is a love story. It opens with the sorrow of death and despair and ends with the joys of marriage and the birth of a son. It is filled with the ordinary events of human life for real people in the ancient world—famine, mourning, gleaning the fields, the search for a husband, the desire for a family. There seems to be nothing supernatural about the story at all. Yet it becomes very clear that God is present and working in people's lives as they respond in faithfulness and generosity in the ordinary circumstances of human life.

In a time of famine a Hebrew couple and their two sons have migrated from Bethlehem to the foreign land of Moab. There they settle and their sons marry Moabite girls. Eventually the father and both sons die, and the mother Naomi decides to return to the land of Judah. She urges her two daughters-in-law to return to their mothers' houses in Moab. Ruth, however, is determined to go with her mother-in-law to Bethlehem. She wants to adopt Naomi's people, her land, and especially her God.

But Ruth said, "Do not press me to go back and abandon you!
> Wherever you go I will go,
>> wherever you lodge I will lodge.
> Your people shall be my people
>> and your God, my God.
> Where you die I will die,
>> and there be buried.
May the LORD do thus to me, and more, if even death separates me from you!" (Ruth 1:16-17)

Ruth accompanies Naomi to Israel and provides for their needs. Living in poverty, Ruth gleans the harvest in the fields of a wealthy relative of Naomi, a man by the name of Boaz of Bethlehem. Ruth catches the attention of Boaz, and he ensures that she is treated well. He praises Ruth for her fidelity to Naomi and for coming to an unknown land: "May you receive a full reward from the LORD, the God of Israel, under whose wings you have come for refuge" (Ruth 2:12). This echo of God's words at Mount Sinai favorably contrasts the fidelity of Ruth to the lack of trust in God shown by many native Israelites.

Eventually Ruth marries the influential Boaz of Bethlehem. Through unwavering trust and faithfulness to God's covenant, a seemingly hopeless situation is brought to a happy ending with the birth of their son. Set in the period of the Judges, the work shows God's concern—not only in caring for widows and responding to human plight, but in using simple human circumstances to prepare for a new stage of salvation history. Ruth, the foreigner, joins herself to the people and the God of Israel, and she becomes the great-grandmother of King David. Through her faith, she is grafted onto the people of Israel and the line of the future messiah.

## The Book of Tobit

Tobit is a story about two Jewish families living in exile in foreign lands. Tobit and Sarah are both righteous people who are unexplainably stricken by misfortune. Tobit has been reduced to poverty and afflicted with blindness. Sarah has lost seven husbands, all of them killed on their wedding night. The story weaves these two families together and becomes a lesson on how to live faithfully in covenant while away from the land of Israel.

Recalling a large sum of money he had deposited in far off Media, Tobit sends his son Tobiah on a long journey to bring back the money. Tobiah is accompanied by an angel in disguise. The angel saves Tobiah from danger, brings about his successful marriage with Sarah, and brings him back home with the money and with a cure for Tobit's blindness.

The story demonstrates that faithfulness to the covenant and virtuous living triumph in the face of adversity. This religious novella encourages all Jews to retain the traditions of their ancestors and the virtues of Judaism: reverence for God, honor for parents, the sacredness of marriage, and the value of almsgiving, fasting, and prayer.

### The Book of Judith

The book of Judith tells the story of a beautiful and courageous woman whose life parallels the history of Israel. She represents defenseless but trusting Israel in the face of the overwhelming power of the other nations. As in the account of Moses and Pharaoh and as in the story of David and Goliath, God defends Israel the underdog. Through this courageous woman, God conquers the armies of the Assyrians.

The Assyrian war machine seems overwhelming. When they realize that only one nation is still opposing them, the Assyrians advance into Israel, striking terror into the hearts of the people. When the Jews become exhausted, with their water supply cut off, and ready to surrender, Judith comes on the scene to urge Israel to resist the enemy and to be confident in God's abiding presence.

Holofernes, the commander of the Assyrian army, is proud, lusty, and arrogant. Judith is humble, beautiful, and single-minded. After praying to God, she departs the city at midnight and enters into the camp of the enemy. When she is captured, the Assyrians are astounded by her beauty, and she wins the confidence of Holofernes. She charms him as they feast in his tent, and when he is in a stupor from drink, she cuts off his head. When his army finds the headless body of their leader, they flee and are pursued and slaughtered by the people of Israel. A rather gruesome account by our standards, but told by ancient Israel as the act of a great hero.

Judith is proud to be an Israelite and she instills that pride in others. She urges the people to be true to their deepest identity as a covenanted people. Her story teaches Israel that God can deliver them from even the worst of times if they trust in God's power and remain faithful to God's covenant. After the victory, the elders of Jerusalem give praise and bless her.

> "You are the glory of Jerusalem!
>   You are the great pride of Israel!
>   You are the great boast of our nation!
> By your own hand you have done all this.
>   You have done good things for Israel,
>   and God is pleased with them.
> May the Almighty Lord bless you forever!"
>   (Judith 15:9-10)

You may have wondered why books such as Tobit and Judith are included in Catholic Bibles but not Protestant Bibles. There are a total of seven such books in the Old Testament: Tobit, Judith, 1–2 Maccabees, Wisdom, Sirach, and Baruch (along with some additions to Esther and Daniel). These books are called **"deuterocanonical"** or "second canon." These books were included in the *Greek translation* of the Hebrew Scriptures (the *Septuagint*), a translation used by early Christians, who adopted all of the books in the *Septuagint* as part of their canon (a set of inspired and approved sacred texts). In the second century A.D., the Jewish canon was formalized, and these seven books were not included. The Protestant Church follows the Jewish canon, while the Catholic Church has maintained the canon of the early church. The New Testament canon is the same for both Protestants and Catholics.

## The Book of Esther

The book of Esther is named after another heroine of Israel. This historical novella is set in the opulent court of the Persian Empire. Esther, a beautiful Jewish woman, becomes the wife of the King of Persia. Her uncle, a devout Jew named Mordecai, displeases a high official of the court and, in retaliation, the official plots to have all the Jews of the empire killed. When Esther discovers the evil plans, she risks her own life to save the lives of her people. The plot is reversed as the official is put to death and Mordecai takes his place.

The story is about reversals, and about God's care for the lives of the people of Israel. Mordecai, a simple exile, becomes the highest court official. Esther, a poor orphaned Jew, becomes the queen. The insignificant Jews earn the respect and fear of the Persians. The story is celebrated each year in the springtime feast of Purim. It is a celebration of Jewish survival and the providence of God watching over them.

## Jonah the Prophet

The story of Jonah is perhaps the most entertaining of the stories. Since Jonah is a prophet, the book is found in the prophetic writings of the Bible. Yet, unlike the other prophetic books, Jonah is clearly a short story, a parable designed to teach as it entertains. The book begins as Jonah is called by God to preach to the people of Nineveh, the capital of the hated Assyrians. Jonah, however, runs away from God and boards a ship headed in the opposite direction.

The ship is threatened with a great storm on the sea, and when the sailors surmise that Jonah is responsible for the storm, he is thrown overboard. Jonah is swallowed by a giant fish, and after three days and three nights he is spewed up by the fish on the shore.

Again God calls Jonah to preach the message of repentance to the people of Nineveh. This time Jonah reluctantly obeys. Incredibly and much to Jonah's disappointment, the king and all the people fast and do penance. As the story ends, Jonah sulks in anger and disbelief as God declares his concern for all the people of Nineveh.

During his journey, Jonah finds himself in environments foreign to him: first the community of sailors, then the people of Assyria. Jonah does not, however, integrate himself into these other communities. He does not engage with those unlike himself, but maintains physical and emotional distance. When the ship is in danger and all hands are working desperately above deck, Jonah goes down to sleep in the hold. When the Ninevites act in response to his prophecy, Jonah goes off by himself and sits outside the city. He does not return others' concern for him or engage others' needs, and by the conclusion of the story, Jonah remains still surly, uncaring, resentful, and isolated.

The non-Israelite sailors and Ninevites respond in an exemplary way to their plight. Although they recognize that the ship and their very lives are in danger because of Jonah's actions, the captain and other sailors only cast their passenger overboard as a last resort and at his own command (Jonah 1:12-16). The Ninevites likewise respond in an exceptionally conscientious and receptive manner toward Jonah and his message. They listen and react immediately to this foreign prophet. Both of these non-Israelite peoples show themselves to be more pious and faithful than the Israelite Jonah.

The sailors respond to their danger by first praying to their gods and asking Jonah to do likewise. They hope that their gods will care for them and keep them safe, and they recognize the wrongness of disobeying a divine directive. But they soon turn to the God of Israel for help, hoping that a deity who is not their own will care about them also. The Ninevites too hope that God will relent so that they will not perish. If they are not outright converted, they clearly recognize Jonah's religion and acknowledge the power of the LORD. "The people of Nineveh believed God," repenting, fasting, and donning sackcloth (Jonah 3:5). The religious understanding of the non-Israelites is superior to that of Jonah.

The story is filled with humor and irony. We can imagine listeners in Israel laughing at the foolishness of Jonah and then realizing that they are just like him in many of their attitudes. Nineveh is that situation in the life of everyone that seems beyond our abilities and our concerns. The God of Israel is a universal god, not nationalistic or otherwise particularistic, kind and compassionate toward all. God spares the sailors' lives and relents in punishing the Ninevites. The book challenges hearers to realize that God's care extends to all the nations and that through people like Jonah, God's promises to Abraham will be fulfilled. Through his descendants, all the nations of the earth will be blessed.

---

Israel's songs and short stories are wonderful reminders to us that a relationship with God involves one's whole life. The songs of Israel demonstrate that human feelings, from fierce anger to ecstatic joy, can be experiences of God's presence. The stories show us how events of human interaction and moments of courage and faithfulness reveal the nearness of God working for us and among us.

## ISRAEL'S WISDOM TRADITION

Parents pass on to their children the wisdom of the family from generation to generation: "Try to choose good friends"; "Learn from your mistakes"; "Honesty is the best policy." Through wisdom like this, parents try to help their children live a good life and make the right choices. We often pass on wisdom in the form of wise sayings: "Look before you leap"; "Don't count your chickens before they hatch"; "Don't put all your eggs in one basket." In easily remembered maxims, we hand on the results of human experience so that others can learn from them.

Strains of wisdom can be found throughout the biblical literature of Israel. But there are several books that may be categorized specifically as wisdom writings. They are the books of Job, Proverbs, Ecclesiastes, Wisdom, and Sirach. These writings are distinctly different from the Pentateuch and the Prophets. Their concern is not primarily about God's revelation, the covenant with God, or the temple and right worship. Their subject matter, rather, is how to live a good life and make good choices in the world of human life and behavior.

### The Teachers of Wisdom

Israel's wise teachers pass on this wisdom in the form of proverbs, parables, allegories, and riddles. They often write as a father counseling his child or as the king giving good advice to his subjects. Often this wisdom consists of short sayings or rhythmic, parallel poetry that can be easily memorized.

The wisdom of Israel is associated with King Solomon, just as the Torah is associated with Moses and the Psalms are associated with King David. Several of the wisdom books are attributed to Solomon since he has become the principal patron of wisdom in Israel. It is highly possible that Solomon wrote some of the wisdom writings, just as Moses wrote some of the Torah and David wrote some of the Psalms. But these three persons are associated with these traditions primarily because their lives embody the best of each literary tradition.

Solomon's reputation for wisdom is widely known. The most famous story of Solomon's wisdom is his encounter with the two women claiming the same baby (1 Kgs 3:16-28). By ordering the child to be cut in two, Solomon shows his understanding of the human heart. He knows that the true mother is the one who is willing to give her child away rather than let the child be harmed. When all the people hear about this, they understand that the king possesses the wisdom of God for giving judgment. The book of 1 Kings further declares that Solomon is wiser than all others and that people come to hear Solomon's wisdom from all nations, sent by all the kings of the earth who have heard of his wisdom.

Later in Israel's history, a class of people who are teachers of wisdom develops alongside the priests and prophets. These three groups—priests, prophets, and sages—deeply influenced the life and thought of the people of Israel. The priests lead worship and interpret the law; the prophets speak God's will centered in the covenant; the sages offer good advice for the issues and problems of the day.

**The Sources of Wisdom**

The Israelites learn much of their wisdom from other wisdom traditions of the ancient world, especially those of Egypt and Mesopotamia. In content, there are many similarities in the wisdom writings of the ancient Middle East. Their advice is about making good choices, living a successful life, dealing well with others, and learning practical solutions to life's problems.

However, biblical wisdom is no mere imitation of the wisdom of other cultures. The biblical writings far transcend their parallels in other cultures in terms of range of thought, originality, and depth of vision. They demonstrate that the poets and sages of Israel both participated in their cultural surroundings and profoundly challenged them.

In addition, the underlying spirit of Israel's wisdom is decidedly different from that of the surrounding cultures. In Israel wisdom is sought through an ever-increasing knowledge of God and of God's will. By reflecting on God's work manifested in the world around them and in human life, the wise sages offer time-tested advice based on human experience and human reason. The sages of Israel realize that a relationship with God involves every area of life, even life's most mundane details.

The sources of Israel's wisdom are twofold. The wise ones attain wisdom first through reflecting on God's revelation found in the Torah and the prophets, and second through meditating on their own experiences of the world and human life. Through both divine revelation and human reason, the sages of Israel are able to communicate and teach the results of their own understanding of God's ways in the realm of human life. They reflect on life's problems and mysteries—such as injustice, happiness and suffering, reward and punishment, our origins and our destiny. They also offer advice for getting along in life—guidance for marriage, family, business, friendships, and social relations.

Wisdom is always related to practice. A person cannot be wise unless that person is also good. Knowledge that is divorced from human life and human action is not wisdom at all. The wise person is described as sensible, understanding, discrete, prudent, and discerning. The person who despises wisdom is depicted as proud, foolish, senseless, wicked, and ignorant. The seat of wisdom in human life is not the mind but the heart. The mark of a wise person is not great intellectual ability, but the ability to make good choices that will order one's life in the way of God.

**Wisdom Personified**

These sources of wisdom are summarized and personified in the image of Lady Wisdom. The learner must make wisdom his companion and lover, forsaking the deception and foolishness of the harlot. The Wisdom Woman (see Prov 8) speaks honestly, sincerely, and truthfully. Her fruit is better than gold and silver. She spreads a table of fine foods and wine, and she invites all to share in her banquet.

Wisdom is of divine origin, begotten of God before creation. She was present with God when he planned the world, established its marvelous order, and embellished it with beauty and variety. She is God's intimate delight, and she invites human beings to this kind of bond with God through a relationship with her.

When he fixed the foundations of earth,
    then was I beside him as artisan;
I was his delight day by day,
    playing before him all the while,
Playing over the whole of his earth,
    having my delight with human beings.
Now, children, listen to me;
    happy are they who keep my ways.
Listen to instruction and grow wise,
    do not reject it! (Prov 8:29-33)

As the word of God, Wisdom comes forth "from the mouth of the Most High" (Sir 24:3). Although she covers the entire earth, from the height of heaven to the deep abyss, she seeks a place to pitch her tent and finds her home in Israel.

"Then the Creator of all gave me his command,
    and my Creator chose the spot for my tent.
He said, 'In Jacob make your dwelling,
    in Israel your inheritance.'
Before all ages, from the beginning, he created me,
    and through all ages I shall not cease to be.
In the holy tent I ministered before him,
    and so I was established in Zion.
In the city he loves as he loves me, he gave me rest;
    in Jerusalem, my domain.
I struck root among the glorious people,
    in the portion of the Lord, his heritage."
        (Sir 24:8-12)

Like a tree, she is planted in Israel and spreads out her glorious branches. Like a vine, she buds forth and produces fruit that is sweeter than honey. Yet, those who partake of her will always desire more. Like a stream, she waters a garden. She grows into a flowing river and then becomes a sea. She pours out her instruction and bestows it far and wide on generations yet to come.

In the book of Wisdom, Solomon describes her as "an unfailing treasure" and praises her incomparable dignity (Wis 7:14). He describes her divine origins and closeness with God.

For she is a breath of the might of God
    and a pure emanation of the glory of the
        Almighty;
    therefore nothing defiled can enter into her.
For she is the reflection of eternal light,
    the spotless mirror of the power of God,
    the image of his goodness. (Wis 7:25-26)

God loves nothing so much as the one who dwells with Wisdom. This is the treasure that sages find when they search out God's inner life and explore God's powerful and eternal word. These images continue into the sacred literature of the New Testament to express the nature of the Christ, "the image of the invisible God, / the firstborn of all creation" (Col 1:15). This is the word of God who was in the beginning with God, through whom all things came to be, who pitched his tent among us (John 1). God now speaks to us through "a son, whom he made heir of all things and through whom he created the universe,"

who is the refulgence of his glory,
    the very imprint of his being,
and who sustains all things by his mighty
        word." (Heb 1:3)

### The Unifying Themes of Wisdom

Each of the wisdom books offers distinctive content, yet there are a number of themes that repeatedly surface. These motifs make the wisdom of Israel distinctive and offer insights that surpass those of surrounding cultures.

1. Israel's wisdom literature declares that *"fear of the Lord" is the beginning of wisdom.* The root of all wisdom is honoring the centrality of God in human life. In God alone is found all wisdom. If a person has wisdom, it is because God has given it as a gift—a gift that is received through

study, discipline, counsel, observation, and reflection.

2. This sacred literature demonstrates how *human wisdom has its limits*. Although the insights gained from human experiences can often deepen one's understanding, these insights are fraught with insecurity and uncertainty. Although human understanding discerns a kind of order inherent in the world, life can never be completely understood or controlled. That dimension of wisdom that explains the inner workings of life is beyond human reach and resides with God alone.

3. Wisdom reflects on *the ways of the just and the wicked in relationship to God*. As the wisdom of the first psalms tell us, "The Lord knows the way of the just, but the way of the wicked leads to ruin." Many proverbs reflect on the behavior of the just and the wicked and the outcomes their actions bring. However, the simple correlation between God's reward for the just and punishment for the wicked does not always seem to hold. The wisdom literature raises the issue of God's justice and reflects on the mystery of evil in the context of faith.

4. The literature speaks of *the need to search for wisdom and obtain it*. Wisdom is elusive and is difficult to find and acquire. Ecclesiastes highlights the futility of seeking wisdom by merely human means, yet Proverbs assures the seeker that the one who searches long enough will find divine wisdom by searching her out like hidden treasure.

5. Wisdom writings wrestle with *the reality of human suffering*. Laments express the physical and spiritual realities of suffering and often express a definitive trust. Yet attempts to explain suffering ultimately fail, and the human experience of suffering can only be accepted in the presence of God.

## The Tale of Job

The book of Job explores some of the most difficult and perplexing questions of religious faith. Why do innocent people suffer? What are we to think when bad things happen to good people? That perplexing problem just won't go away and is still with us in many forms today.

In this drama, the author uses an ancient legendary hero, Job, as the protagonist. Job is a good and prosperous man who has lived blamelessly before God. But suddenly he suffers a complete reversal of fortune: he loses his property and his children, his body is afflicted with a disease, and he is plagued with deep depression.

The core of the drama consists of three cycles of speeches forming a debate between Job and his friends. Job argues that life is unfair. He curses the day of his birth and longs for death, yet all the while he defends his complete innocence before God. Job's friends represent the traditional answers. They insist that his suffering must be the result of some personal sin and they urge him to repent before God.

The author of Job is challenging the traditional wisdom of Israel. Since the early days, God's people were satisfied with the simple assurance that God is good and just. Therefore, as Deuteronomy says, those who love God and walk in God's ways will have a long and prosperous life. However, those who turn away from God will perish. When life goes well for people, it is a sign that they are living a good life; when things go badly, surely the person has sinned against God and God has responded with affliction. God punishes the wicked and rewards the good. As right as that might seem to human reason, the author knows that is not always the way it works.

The climax of the drama occurs as Job rejects the answers of his friends and cries out in anger to God, demanding an account of God's actions. God the Almighty, the Creator of all, is being put on the witness stand by Job in his tiny little corner of the great universe. Job has tested God's wisdom. So God addresses Job out of the storm. God does not give Job any answers; rather God questions Job. Where were you when I created the universe? Can you control the powers of the seas or the heavens? Can you understand the ways of birth and death in all the living creatures of the earth? The questions pour forth from God relentlessly. Like a good teacher, God questions Job in order to lead him to new insights.

Then God exclaims: "Let him who would correct God give answer!" (Job 40:2). Job's inability to comprehend or control the created world helps him realize that there is much in his own life that he will never be able to completely comprehend or to fully control.

Job responds with humility before God who is all-wise and all-powerful, indicating that he has learned the lesson that God is trying to teach him.

> Then Job answered the LORD and said:
> I know that you can do all things,
>   and that no purpose of yours can be
>     hindered.
> "Who is this who obscures counsel with
>     ignorance?"
> I have spoken but did not understand;
>   things too marvelous for me, which I did not
>     know.
> "Listen, and I will speak;
> I will question you, and you tell me the
>     answers."
> By hearsay I had heard of you,
>   but now my eye has seen you.
> Therefore I disown what I have said,
>   and repent in dust and ashes. (Job 42:1-6)

Job's questions have not been answered. The questions are too big; human logic fails in the face of the almighty God. The presence of such mystery does not call for questions, but for humble faith. Job must trust in God's wisdom and not claim the right to know what God does not choose to reveal.

The book of Job teaches us that in times of suffering and loss, our logic falls short. We cannot offer simplistic answers to life's problems. Statements like, "If you have enough faith in God, you will be cured" still do a lot of harm and place unnecessary guilt on people. We cannot presume to know the secrets of God's wisdom. Only an awareness that God is with us in our pain can bring comfort.

## The Anthology of Proverbs

The book of Proverbs is an anthology of wisdom writings. The collected works are directed primarily to the young and inexperienced, but also to those who desire advanced instruction in wisdom. The writings contain the distilled wisdom of centuries of experience and observation. Two of the several collections are attributed to Solomon and could possibly date back to his reign.

The proverbs cover a broad range of human affairs and teach a multitude of lessons. Generally the proverbs contain practical, down-to-earth advice about how to live well, how to make responsible, successful choices in life. The proverbs teach what might be called "old fashioned basic values." They warn against greed, laziness, infidelity, and dishonesty. They encourage discipline, moderation, respect for authority, and concern for the needy.

While most of the proverbs deal with what we might call everyday life, at the root of them all is one's relationship with God: "The beginning of wisdom is fear of the LORD, / and knowledge of the Holy One is understanding" (Prov 9:10). Fear of God is not a trembling dread, but rather a sense of awe and reverence before God which leads to following God's instructions and seeking God's will.

A few guidelines will help in reading the book of Proverbs. First, proverbs are designed to give brief, practical advice. Second, they are phrased to be catchy and easily learned. Third, they are intended to be read together and balanced by one another. Fourth, they reflect the practices of an ancient culture. Fifth, they use metaphor, exaggeration, and other techniques to express their truth.

So, when we read the proverbs, we should not expect them to be complete statements of truth that apply to every situation. For example, Proverbs counsels, "Entrust your works to the LORD, / and your plans will succeed" (16:3).

73

This does not offer a guarantee for success in every situation of life. It expresses, rather, the more general truth that when our lives are committed to God, we will succeed according to God's understanding of success. The proverbs are guidelines for making decisions in life, but they are not exhaustive for every time and every situation. Often the proverbs will need to be applied to our own lives by peeling away the literary form and the cultural situation of ancient Israel to find the essential truth.

## The Quest of Ecclesiastes

The book of Ecclesiastes stands in sharp contrast to the optimism of the book of Proverbs. Like the book of Job, Ecclesiastes challenges the easy answers of popular wisdom. The work is not based on worn-out and pious platitudes about how life is supposed to be, but on real-life experience and observation. In this very honest view of human life, the author demonstrates how impossible it is to discern the plan of God.

The book is written by a Jewish sage who calls himself Qoheleth. It is not a cohesive narrative or systematic presentation; it is more like a notebook of reflections. The writer is constantly probing and asking questions of life. And after reviewing all the things that are often thought to make people happy—wealth, knowledge, pleasure—he comes to the conclusion that nothing in life brings lasting satisfaction.

Qoheleth compares human life to the natural world to make his point. In the cycles of nature, nothing is really accomplished. There is a sense of incompleteness in all things.

> One generation departs and another generation comes,
>  but the world forever stays.
> The sun rises and the sun sets;
>  then it presses on to the place where it rises.
> Shifting south, then north,
>  back and forth shifts the wind, constantly shifting its course.
> All rivers flow to the sea,
>  yet never does the sea become full.

> To the place where they flow,
>  the rivers continue to flow. (Eccl 1:4-7)

The recurring theme of the book is the vanity of all things: "Vanity of vanities, says Qoheleth, / vanity of vanities! All things are vanity!" (Eccl 1:2). Everything in human life is futile, useless, and empty. We work all our life and what do we have to show for it? Seeking wisdom, the writer says, is like chasing after the wind. Seeking pleasure doesn't lead to any lasting satisfaction. Accumulated wealth is only a cause of worry that won't let us sleep. The wise person and the fool, the just person and the wicked—they all end up in the grave. The writer is resigned to the difficult and often cruel facts of life.

The reflections of Qoheleth are unsettling and troubling, sometimes even shocking, to the person of faith. Yet the author maintains the utmost reverence toward God. He always asserts that God is good, just, and wise; but he claims that we cannot understand the meaning of God's work. Qoheleth, like Job before him, searches for meaning in life, yet acknowledges that it is beyond human grasp.

As the sun moves from one end of the sky to the other and as the wind shifts continually back and forth, so human activity is forever oscillating from one extreme to another. The contrasting moments of life all have their appropriate time and place within the providence of God.

> There is an appointed time for everything,
>  and a time for every affair under the heavens.
> A time to give birth, and a time to die;
>  a time to plant, and a time to uproot the plant.
> A time to kill, and a time to heal;
>  a time to tear down, and a time to build.
> A time to weep, and a time to laugh;
>  a time to mourn, and a time to dance.
> A time to scatter stones, and a time to gather them;
>  a time to embrace, and a time to be far from embraces.
> A time to seek, and a time to lose;
>  a time to keep, and a time to cast away.
> A time to rend, and a time to sew;
>  a time to be silent, and a time to speak.

A time to love, and a time to hate;
    a time of war, and a time of peace. (Eccl 3:1-8)

We can step back from the immediacy of life at times and glimpse the totality. Yet, we can never grasp or control our lives. Although we yearn for direction and power over our lives, we do not shape or determine our lives. We cannot discern the meaning of it all or its overarching plan. Although life holds its moments of joy and pleasures, it holds no lasting, secure happiness. Nothing in life can truly satisfy the longings of the human heart.

Only the present moment, Qoheleth concludes, can offer human existence any sense of meaning. Satisfaction can only be found in the very act of living each day. Reverence and respect for God's sovereignty prompts a life of simplicity in deeds and integrity in words. In the final analysis, Qoheleth urges his listeners to live well because all people are responsible for their actions. God's judgment brings all things to light, both our deeds and our hidden motives.

The last word, when all is heard: Fear God and keep his commandments, for this concerns all humankind; because God will bring to judgment every work, with all its hidden qualities, whether good or bad. (Eccl 12:13-14)

We've all felt like Qoheleth at times; we've felt discouraged, confused, and hopeless about life. When we realize that nothing in this world is lasting, it forces us to raise the same questions as Qoheleth. While these reflections in the book of Ecclesiastes are not pleasant reading, they are thought provoking. All the questions it raises really ask the same thing: "What is there of ultimate value that makes life worthwhile?" Qoheleth does not give us any resolution. Ultimately, Ecclesiastes is a book of questions waiting for answers.

Belief in the resurrection of the dead and fullness of life with God had not yet developed at the time of Qoheleth. The common understanding was that all of the dead went to a place of rest called **Sheol**. Existence in Sheol was little better than suspended animation. There was no pain, no joy, no memory, no communication, no light. Belief in the resurrection of the dead began to develop in the mid-second century B.C.

## The Search for True Wisdom

The book of Wisdom is written very late in biblical history. Perhaps it is the last Old Testament book to be written. It is written at a time in which the Jews are scattered into many parts of the Greek world and are heavily influenced by Hellenist philosophy and ways of thought. Many abandon their Jewish faith and many of those who remain faithful are persecuted.

The author of Wisdom wants to show Jewish readers that true wisdom is found in God's revelation to Israel, not in the pagan ways of Greek culture. While the author uses the Greek language and the more abstract Greek terminology, the teachings are formed from the ancient faith of Israel.

The first five chapters of Wisdom treat the question of human destiny. The question arises from the perplexing problem of innocent suffering, already treated by Job and Ecclesiastes. For the author of Wisdom, answers are found not only in this life, but in life after death. The author declares that the just will be rewarded and the wicked punished, if not in this life, then in the life to come. The book contains the clearest Old Testament teaching on eternal life.

But the righteous live forever,
    and in the LORD is their recompense,
    and the thought of them is with the Most High.
Therefore shall they receive the splendid crown,
    the beautiful diadem, from the hand of the LORD,
For he will shelter them with his right hand,
    and protect them with his arm. (Wis 5:15-16)

In the next part of the book, the author places the teachings on the lips of the wise King Solomon. He praises wisdom, teaching its origin and nature, and how it can be acquired. Using language that any Greek could appreciate, the author proclaims that wisdom is a sharing in the very nature of God.

> For in her is a spirit
> > intelligent, holy, unique,
> Manifold, subtle, agile,
> > clear, unstained, certain,
> Never harmful, loving the good, keen,
> > unhampered, beneficent, kindly,
> Firm, secure, tranquil,
> > all-powerful, all-seeing,
> And pervading all spirits,
> > though they be intelligent, pure and very
> > > subtle. (Wis 7:22-23)

These twenty-one characteristics of wisdom are borrowed from Greek philosophy and mythology. They resemble the attributes associated with Isis, the pagan goddess of wisdom. Yet the sage makes certain that these qualities of wisdom are also divine qualities of Israel's God. The spirit of wisdom is also the spirit of the Lord. These attributes of wisdom that pervade the Greek culture are the same qualities that God poured out at creation to rule the world and direct it in fulfilling the divine will.

The last part of the work is a reflection on Israel's history, showing God's wisdom guiding the people of God. The author reflects on the earliest history of Israel, focusing especially on the experience of Exodus. It takes the form of a homiletic midrash, a method of Jewish interpretation that makes the traditional narratives relevant in new situations. In this way, the Torah provides faithful direction to a new generation. Showing that God's wisdom preserved Israel during the time of slavery in Egypt, the author expresses the hope that God's people will always follow the way of wisdom when they are in foreign lands and during times of persecution.

## The Wisdom of Sirach

The final wisdom writing in the Old Testament canon is the book of Sirach. It is one of the longest books of the Bible and is the largest collection of wisdom writings. The author is a sage who lives in Jerusalem and conducts a school there for young Jews seeking wisdom. He says that during his younger life he traveled and studied the Torah, the Prophets, and the writings of Israel. In his later years he writes down much of his acquired wisdom to help the Jewish people maintain and appreciate their ancient faith and tradition in the face of the Greek culture around them.

Like the book of Proverbs, Sirach is a collection of practical instructions. Unlike Proverbs, which is a random collection of sayings, Sirach is arranged according to subjects. Among its many topics are duty to parents, social conduct, friendship, family life, the use of wealth, religious worship, and table etiquette. His work is full of common sense, with a deep respect for the traditions handed down through the ages.

In the final chapters, the author praises God's great deeds and Israel's great heroes throughout history. This is evidence that God's wisdom had indeed pitched her tent among God's people. In a culture that threatens the ancient faith, Sirach recommends that the young people of Israel look to their ancestors for wisdom and guidance, as models to be imitated.

---

The books of Israel's wisdom are much like the advice of loving grandparents—people who have experienced lots of life and have learned a lot in the process. They urge us to respect the wisdom of the past and to be patient with what we cannot understand. They advise us to avoid simplistic answers to the complex questions of life and to build our lives on the timeless truths that God has revealed through the ages.

**EXPLORING LESSON THREE**

1. Revisit Lesson Two for a few moments. When you consider the sweep of Israel's history in the Old Testament period, what themes, ideas or events stand out to you as particularly important?

_____

_____

_____

_____

2. How would you describe the psalms? How are they different from the biblical material we have studied so far?

_____

_____

_____

_____

3. Many psalms recount the mighty deeds of God among his people (e.g., Psalms 78; 105; 107; 135). How might we find it helpful in our own spiritual lives to recall God's "mighty deeds"—or the ways God has acted in our own lives?

_____

_____

_____

_____

4. a) What types of prayers are included in the book of Psalms?

_____

_____

_____

b) How are the prayers of lament—which may express anger with God, a sense of abandonment, and even a desire for revenge—a healthy part of an honest dialogue with God?

_____

_____

_____

_____

5. What is the Song of Songs about? How did Israel understand this love poem?

_____

_____

_____

_____

6. Choose one of Israel's short stories (Ruth, Tobit, Judith, Esther, or Jonah). What lessons are taught by this story? Why would these lessons have been important to the Israelite people? Why are they important to you?

_____

_____

_____

_____

7. What is the main subject matter or focus of the wisdom writings (Job, Proverbs, Ecclesiastes, Wisdom, and Sirach)? What was the role of Israel's sages?

_____

_____

_____

_____

8. How did Israelite wisdom differ from the wisdom traditions of the ancient world such as that of Egypt and Mesopotamia?

_____

_____

_____

_____

9. a) In what way does the book of Job challenge the traditional wisdom of Israel about human suffering?

_____

_____

_____

b) What wisdom does this book share about suffering?

_____

_____

_____

10. After reading about the unique book of Ecclesiastes, what do you find compelling about this book? Which of Qoheleth's observations resonate with you? Are you surprised to find this kind of wisdom in the Bible?

_____

_____

_____

_____

## CLOSING PRAYER

*Prayer*

*O God, you are my God—*
*it is you I seek!*
*For you my body yearns;*
*for you my soul thirsts,*
*In a land parched, lifeless,*
*and without water.*
*I look to you in the sanctuary*
*to see your power and glory.*
*For your love is better than life;*
*my lips shall ever praise you!*
(Ps 63:2-4)

God of Wisdom, we seek you in our everyday experiences and relationships. We seek you in the sanctuary, at work, and at home. Fill us with your wisdom that we may recognize your loving presence in all places and in all experiences. We pray this week for those who are most in need of your wisdom and presence, especially . . .

# LESSON FOUR

## The Prophetic Books

Begin your personal study and group discussion with a simple and sincere prayer such as:

*Prayer*

*Loving God, you liberated your people and led them to the Promised Land. Liberate our minds and hearts as we study your word, that we may live joyfully as your faithful people.*

Read pages 82–98, Lesson Four.

Respond to the questions on pages 99–100, Exploring Lesson Four.

The Closing Prayer on page 101 is for your personal use and may be used at the end of group discussion.

## CHALLENGING THE TIMES

The relationship between King David and the prophet Nathan demonstrates the role of the prophet in Israel's history. King David has taken the beautiful Bathsheba from her loving husband and committed adultery with her. David then schemes to have her husband killed in battle and takes her as his wife. So God sends the prophet Nathan to David, and the prophet challenges the king with a parable.

> The LORD sent Nathan to David, and when he came to him, he said: "Tell me how you judge this case: In a certain town there were two men, one rich, the other poor. The rich man had flocks and herds in great numbers. But the poor man had nothing at all except one little ewe lamb that he had bought. He nourished her, and she grew up with him and his children. Of what little he had she ate; from his own cup she drank; in his bosom she slept; she was like a daughter to him. Now, a visitor came to the rich man, but he spared his own flocks and herds to prepare a meal for the traveler who had come to him: he took the poor man's ewe lamb and prepared it for the one who had come to him." (2 Sam 12:1-4)

David grows angry and he says to Nathan, "The man who has done this deserves death!" Then Nathan looks at David and says, "You are the man!" And David is brought to repentance.

### The Role of a Prophet in Israel

This is the role of the prophet: to challenge, to chastise, and to call to repentance and conversion. The prophets are the conscience of Israel. They never win any popularity contests. They upset people; they say things that people don't want to hear. Frequently the prophets are persecuted because their words run counter to so many of the vested interests of their day.

The prophet in Israel is not one who foretells the future like a fortune-teller, as is sometimes assumed today. Rather, the role of the prophet in essence is to speak on behalf of God, to communicate "the word of the LORD."

Prophets are concerned primarily with current events, with their own historical situation before God. The task of the prophets is to tell how God sees things—in the past or in the future, but especially in the present.

The prophets do not come from any particular group or class of people. They are shepherds, farmers, scribes, noblemen, and priests. They speak in the temple, in the king's palace, in the marketplace, or at the city gates—wherever they believe they will be effective. But what they all have in common is their call to speak to the people of Israel as God's messengers. Divine inspiration makes a person a prophet and causes the prophet to speak out.

Although Abraham (Gen 20:7), Miriam (Exod 15:20), Moses (Deut 34:10), and Deborah (Judg 4:4) are named as prophets in the earlier periods, the role of prophet in Israel's developing statehood begins with the ministry of Samuel. He is a judge and a priest, but he is also a prophet in that he is the one who perceives God's will and speaks the divine will to God's people. He anoints Saul as king, but he is also the sharpest critic of the monarchy in Israel.

The role of the prophet develops alongside the monarchy, and political action is characteristic of the prophets. The king can usually depend on the prophet to tell him what he doesn't want to hear. Nathan is David's court prophet, rebuking the king when he strays from the

LORD's ways. Nathan also plays an active role in Solomon's succession to the throne.

During the declining days of Solomon's reign, the prophet Ahijah prophesies to Jeroboam that the kingdom will be divided because of Solomon's sins. In a dramatic act, the prophet tears his garment into twelve pieces and proclaims that God will tear ten of those parts from Solomon's kingdom and give them to King Jeroboam in the north.

## The Prophets Elijah and Elisha

After the division of the kingdom, the prophets Elijah and Elisha become two of the most memorable figures in Israel. The reign of King Ahab of the northern kingdom forms the backdrop for the career of these men. The confrontation begins as Ahab and his pagan wife Jezebel bring fertility liturgies and sacred prostitution into Samaria. They erect a temple to the Canaanite god Baal and an idol to the goddess Asherah.

Elijah denounces their idolatry and announces a severe drought upon the land. When the land lies devastated, Elijah challenges Ahab and the 450 prophets of Baal to a contest on Mount Carmel. Two altars are prepared on the mountain with two bulls for sacrifice. The competition will demonstrate who is the real God of fertility, the genuine Lord of life.

Although the odds of 450 to 1 don't look good, Elijah addresses the people, "How long will you straddle the issue? If the LORD is God, follow him; if Baal, follow him" (1 Kgs 18:21). So, the pagan prophets invoke their gods to bring down fire upon the altar, but their incantations bring no results. Baal, who is known as the god of fire and lightning, cannot generate a single spark. After many hours of calling and pleading, there is no sound, no one answering, no one listening.

Then Elijah prepares the altar for sacrifice and pours jars of water over the wood. Elijah calls out to the LORD, and God answers him. God sends a great fire from heaven that consumes the sacrifice and the altar. As in the exodus and in all other encounters with the LORD, God answers

and brings redemption. Like Moses who demonstrated God's power over the gods of Egypt, Elijah does wondrous deeds in God's name so that all will know the LORD. The people turn back to God, and the narrative ends as abundant rains come to water the parched land.

Escaping the wrath of Jezebel, Elijah journeys southward for forty days and nights to Mount Horeb (Sinai). Yet, Elijah does not experience God's voice amidst the earthquake, storm, and fire as did Moses, but the prophet listens and God speaks to him through "a light silent sound" (1 Kgs 19:12). For Israel, the two figures of Moses and Elijah sum up the whole of salvation history. Moses represents the Torah and Elijah embodies the prophets. In fact, Israel's prophetic tradition teaches that the age of the messiah will bring a prophet like Moses and the return of Elijah.

At the end of his life, Elijah arrives with Elisha at the Jordan River. Elijah strikes the river with his mantle and the waters part. The two prophets cross over on dry land, just as the Israelites passed into the land many centuries before. Elijah is then taken to heaven in a fiery chariot after passing a double portion of his spirit to his successor Elisha, just as Moses appointed Joshua to carry on his leadership. Elisha takes up the mantle that Elijah has left behind and continues his prophetic ministry to Israel. The Jewish tradition awaits Elijah's return by setting him a place at table and pouring him a cup of wine at every Passover.

 Many of the stories about **Elisha's ministry** describe his miracles for those in need. Miracles are a sign of God's presence and power to banish evil. Some of these stories are paralleled in the Gospels, especially in Luke: raising the widow's son from the dead (2 Kgs 4:18-37; Luke 7:11-16), multiplying the loaves (1 Kgs 4:42-44; Luke 9:10-17 and parallels; also Matt 15:32-38; Mark 8:1-9; John 6:1-13), curing the leper(s) (1 Kgs 5:1-14; Luke 5:12-16 and parallels; Luke 17:11-19). In Luke, Jesus also compares himself to Elijah and Elisha with regard to helping foreigners (Luke 4:25-27).

## The Classical Prophets

The latter prophets, sometimes called the "classical" prophets, are those whose prophecies have been written down and are now part of the biblical canon. Though we have only scattered segments preserved from the earlier prophets, we have extensive collections of these latter prophets that were collected and edited by their disciples.

These prophetic books are divided into the four major prophets—Isaiah, Jeremiah, Ezekiel, and Daniel—and the twelve minor prophets—Hosea, Joel, Amos, Obadiah, Jonah, Micah, Nahum, Habakkuk, Zephaniah, Haggai, Zechariah, and Malachi. These prophetic books are not placed in chronological order in the Bible. The first four prophets are called major prophets simply because their books are the longest. The twelve prophetic books that follow are called minor because their works are comparatively shorter.

The people of Israel realize that the role of prophet is divinely instituted just as that of king and priest. Because of the frequent failure of Israel's kings and priests to keep the covenant alive, Israel needs the prophets as an enduring voice to challenge Israel's leaders, to warn the people of the ruin threatened by infidelity to the covenant, and to call the nation to repentance and authentic worship.

Most of Israel's prophets are associated in one way or another with the reign of the kings. Often the beginning of a prophetic book indicates the name of the reigning king during the time of the prophet's ministry. The prophets begin to speak out in times of political and religious crisis. So it is helpful to know something about the historical context of the period in order to understand better the words of the prophet. We have already seen that the earlier prophets speak out during the united period of the monarchy: Samuel during the reign of Saul, Nathan during David's reign, and Ahijah during the reign of Solomon. Beginning with the division of the kingdom, Elijah and Elisha prophesy during the reign of King Ahab in the ninth century in the northern kingdom.

The period of the classical prophets begins in the eighth century with Amos and Hosea. They prophesy against unfaithfulness and injustice during the reign of Jeroboam II in the northern kingdom. Shortly thereafter, Isaiah and Micah begin to proclaim God's word in the southern kingdom during the reigns of Uzziah, Jotham, Ahaz, and Hezekiah.

| | | Kings and *Prophets* | | |
|---|---|---|---|---|
| 1000 B.C. | | Saul | | *Samuel* |
| | | David | | *Nathan* |
| | | Solomon | | *Ahijah* |
| | **Israel** | | **Judah** | |
| | Jeroboam I | | Rehoboam | |
| 900 | Baasha | | Asa | |
| | Omri | | Jehoshaphat | |
| | Ahab | *Elijah* | | |
| | Jehu | *Elisha* | Jehoash | |
| 800 | | | Amaziah | |
| | Jeroboam II | *Amos* | Uzziah | |
| | | *Hosea* | Jotham | *Isaiah* |
| | Menahem | | Ahaz | *Micah* |
| | Hoshea | | | |
| | **Fall of Samaria** | | | |
| 700 | | | Hezekiah | |
| | | | Manasseh | |
| | | | Josiah | *Zephaniah* |
| | | | | *Jeremiah* |
| | | | | *Nahum* |
| | | | Jehoiakim | *Habbakuk* |
| 600 | | | Zedekiah | |
| | | | **Fall of Jerusalem** | |
| | | | **Exile** | *Ezekiel* |
| | | | | *2 Isaiah* |

The seventh-century prophets—Jeremiah, Zephaniah, Habakkuk, and Naham—are all associated with the kingdom of Judah. They speak out during the reigns of the last kings of Judah, leading up to the destruction of Jerusalem and the Babylonian exile.

The political circumstances within which the prophets speak influence whether they offer a message of accusation and condemnation or a word of hope and encouragement. Generally, the preexilic prophets offer messages of doom, while postexilic prophecies are oracles of salvation.

## True and False Prophets

The legitimacy of individual prophets is difficult to verify. Although the kings and priests are validated for the most part through succession from one generation to the next, those who hear the prophets realize that there is no easy way of making distinctions between true and false prophets. So the principal means of authentication is the content of the message itself.

True prophecy calls people back to Israel's covenant with God. The authentic prophet is faithful to Israel's traditional faith. The false prophets claim to speak for God, but they do not speak the word of the LORD or reflect God's character. They express the voice of those who try to manipulate or control God.

Another criterion for discerning a true prophet is moral courage. A genuine prophet speaks out against injustice and unfaithfulness in the face of opposition and persecution. Legitimate prophets oppose unfaithful kings and they do not compromise the faith of Israel. They challenge people to accountability for their choices. False prophets, on the other hand, are timid and they accommodate their message to the desires of the king. Anyone who promises peace and prosperity to an apostate nation is understood to be a deceiver.

Micah the prophet declares himself filled with God's spirit and with justice. Therefore he declares that Jerusalem and its temple will be reduced to rubble. He addresses the false prophets in the city who mislead the people because their words can be bought.

> Its leaders render judgment for a bribe,
>     the priests teach for pay,
>     the prophets divine for money,
> While they rely on the LORD, saying,
>     "Is not the LORD in the midst of us?
>     No evil can come upon us!"
> Therefore, because of you,
>     Zion shall be plowed like a field,
>     and Jerusalem reduced to rubble,
> And the mount of the temple
>     to a forest ridge. (Mic 3:11-12)

A final quality of authentic prophets is their own subjective certainty about their call to prophecy. They are able to recount how God has called them to prophecy. With a deep inner certitude they know that God has called them to this task, despite their own reluctance.

## The Prophets' Call

The call of the prophet is a mysterious, often unwilling encounter with the living God. In describing his surprising vocation from God, Amos says, "The LORD took me from following the flock, and the LORD said to me, 'Go, prophesy to my people Israel'" (Amos 7:15). He says that the call is so inescapable that it is like the instinctive fear one feels when a lion roars (Amos 3:8).

Isaiah the prophet describes his own calling as a mystical experience, far deeper than anything that can be communicated through the senses. While in the smoke-filled temple of Jerusalem, he sees God on his throne, between the six-winged seraphim. Isaiah is filled with dread because of the wide breach between God's holiness and his own sinfulness.

> Then one of the seraphim flew to me, holding an ember which he had taken with tongs from the altar.
> He touched my mouth with it. "See," he said, "now that this has touched your lips, your wickedness is removed, your sin purged."

Then I heard the voice of the Lord saying,
"Whom shall I send? Who will go for us?"
"Here I am," I said; "send me!" (Isa 6:6-8)

The prophet Jeremiah hears God's voice say to him, "Before I formed you in the womb I knew you, / before you were born I dedicated you, / a prophet to the nations I appointed you" (Jer 1:5). But Jeremiah tries to refuse God's call saying, "I do not know how to speak. I am too young." Then the prophet narrates his commission from the Lord.

But the LORD answered me,
Do not say, "I am too young."
    To whomever I send you, you shall go;
    whatever I command you, you shall speak.
Do not be afraid of them,
    for I am with you to deliver you—oracle of
        the LORD.

Then the LORD extended his hand and touched
    my mouth, saying to me,

See, I place my words in your mouth!
    Today I appoint you
    over nations and over kingdoms,
To uproot and to tear down,
    to destroy and to demolish,
    to build and to plant. (Jer 1:7-10)

Jeremiah's ministry will encompass words of doom, prophesying the destruction of the kingdom, as well as oracles of salvation, delivering God's promise "to build and to plant." Jeremiah realizes that there is no escaping God's call, describing God's word as a fire burning in his heart, imprisoned in his bones (Jer 20:9). This assurance of God's call gives each prophet a sense of conviction and certainty in speaking God's word, and this vocational assurance gives him confidence throughout his ministry of the supportive presence of God. The encounter with God in this mysterious but powerful call changes the prophet's way of looking at reality. With such deep insights into God's will the prophet is no longer able to be comfortable with compromise. He is no longer able to accept a careless relationship with God and a lax response to God's will in the life of the nation.

## The Prophets' Message

The essential message of the prophets is a call to faithfulness to the covenant. In this sense, the prophets are traditionalists. They call God's people back to this relationship of love to which the LORD called Israel so long ago. This fidelity to the covenant can be divided into two fundamental themes that seem to encompass the entire message of the prophets: first, worship of YHWH alone; and second, justice toward others. And these two themes are bound together under the theme of relationship. Both an exclusive relationship with God and inclusive relationships with people are necessary for a faithful response to the covenant.

The LORD is the only God of Israel. The prophets resist any attempts to combine the worship of the one God with devotion to other gods. They employ numerous images to express the deep love that the LORD has for Israel. Parent, teacher, king, shepherd, healer—these are all images that express the tender and passionate care God has for the chosen people. The prophets insist that God is a jealous God who demands faithfulness in their loving relationship. Hosea, among others, compares God's love for Israel with the love of husband and wife. Even though Israel is unfaithful and strays, God's covenant remains and God calls Israel back with a love that does not give up.

The prophets teach that genuine worship of God requires the right treatment of one's fellow human beings, demonstrating how intimately worship and justice are bound together. The prophets speak out in anger when they see the poor being ignored while the rituals of worship are being executed with meticulous care. Worship that is not linked to proper behavior toward one's neighbor is an outrage.

The monarchy in Israel encourages and sometimes even causes much of this deviation from the covenant. As the kingdom of Israel grows and prospers, the kings allow Israelite culture to become increasingly compromised by the influences of other nations. Pagan worship, images, and values begin to chip away at the purity and uniqueness of God's covenant with Israel. The development of social and economic classes leads to divisions among people and to oppression of the poor. The wealthy grow more prosperous, profiting from the labor and exploitation of the lower classes. The prophets know that this kind of compromise deteriorates the very soul of Israel.

The aim of the prophets is always to call people to conversion, to a radical inner change that manifests itself in outwardly reformed deeds. This kind of conversion involves people's minds, hearts, and behaviors. This inner change means turning back to a covenant relationship with God, which is a matter of one's thinking, willing, and acting.

people are headed because of their disobedience to the covenant (Jer 19:10-11). Later, Jeremiah is instructed by God to purchase a plot of land. He puts away the deed to the land for safekeeping until the day he will need to show it in order to verify his ownership of the land. This symbolic action is God's assurance that, after the Babylonian invasion, Judah will be restored and daily life, with its buying and selling, will return to normal.

In all of these expressive actions, the prophets embody their prophecies. They indicate God's will and effect its implementation. The symbolic acts, along with their words, express divine messages, offering both warnings and promises to the people.

## The Words and Deeds of the Prophets

The prophets use many different means to persuade their audiences to believe and to live out their beliefs. On the one hand, the prophets threaten, warn, and announce punishment; on the other hand, the prophets exhort, entice, and promise deliverance. Through metaphors, similes, parables, exaggerations, puns, and other forms of imaginative language, the prophets seek to create change in their hearers by means of language, especially the language of poetry.

In addition to speaking words of prophecy, the prophets often act out their prophecy in gestures. As Saul tears Samuel's garment, the prophet tells Saul that God has torn the kingdom from him (1 Sam 15:27-28). Ahijah's rending his new cloak into twelve pieces expresses the division of Solomon's kingdom (1 Kgs 11:30-32). Isaiah walks naked and barefoot as a captive in order to dramatize the shame of exile that threatens the people (Isa 20:2-4).

Jeremiah gathers some of the nobles of Jerusalem and brings them out to the valley, which serves as the city's trash dump. Bringing with him a large clay pot, he raises it over his head in the sight of all and hurls it to the ground where it smashes to bits. This gesture serves as a powerful prophecy about where the

## Amos and Hosea

The prophet Amos, the earliest of the classical prophets, carries out his prophetic calling in a period of great material prosperity and terrible moral decay in the northern kingdom of Israel. The peasant farmers have been the mainstay of the nation, but now they are being oppressed because of the greed of the wealthy landowners. Their poverty forces them to relinquish family land holdings, allowing the wealthy to amass huge estates. Judges are now making decisions based on the bribes offered by the rich. In the midst of this system of great injustice, religious devotion flourishes. Worshipers offer expensive sacrifices, and the sanctuary of Bethel overflows with pilgrims. Amos denounces this disregard for the social implications of the covenant and announces impending doom for Israel.

> I hate, I despise your feasts,
>   I take no pleasure in your solemnities.
> Even though you bring me your burnt
>     offerings and grain offerings
>   I will not accept them;
> Your stall-fed communion offerings,
>   I will not look upon them.
> Take away from me
>   your noisy songs;
> The melodies of your harps,
>   I will not listen to them.

Rather let justice surge like waters,
and righteousness like an unfailing stream.
(Amos 5:21-24)

Like all the prophets that follow him, Amos preaches about the necessary connections between worshipping God and doing justice to neighbor. Right conduct leads to right worship; ritual sacrifice presumes social justice.

The prophet Hosea speaks God's word to Israel in the same period as Amos. He deplores Israel's worship of the Canaanite fertility gods. These religions believe that the fruitfulness of the crops depends on the sexual coupling of Baal and Asherah. The people suppose that they can benefit from these life-giving powers if they participate in the sexual union through the temple prostitutes.

Hosea grows to understand his own problematic marriage as a pattern for God's relationship with Israel. Hosea's wife becomes repeatedly unfaithful in their marriage; nevertheless, Hosea never stops loving her. He remains determined to woo her back to himself. The way that Hosea responds to his wife becomes an acted-out prophecy, demonstrating the manner in which God will interact with Israel.

Because of the many-layered meaning of poetry, the words of the prophet can be read on two levels: his own marital tragedy and the breakdown of Israel's covenant relationship with God. Hosea's marital drama moves from the intimate relationship of marriage, through infidelity, to divorce, and eventually to reconciliation and reunion. The prophecy moves from covenant union through idolatry, to punishment, and then to reconciliation and a new covenant.

In the midst of Israel's injustice, idolatry, and immorality, Hosea seeks to convince the nation that Israel can return to the faithful marriage of the covenant.

I will betroth you to me forever:
I will betroth you to me with justice and with judgment,
with loyalty and with compassion;
I will betroth you to me with fidelity,
and you shall know the LORD. (Hos 2:21-22)

## Isaiah and Micah

Isaiah, the first of the classical prophets of the southern kingdom of Judah, is a cultured nobleman, advisor to the kings, and an inspiring poet. He describes his prophetic calling as a vision of God in the temple of Jerusalem. Isaiah is overcome with the majestic holiness of God: "Holy, holy, holy is the LORD of hosts! / All the earth is filled with his glory!" (Isa 6:3)

The great gulf between God's holiness and the sinful corruption of God's people overwhelms Isaiah throughout his long ministry. Prophesying during the reign of four kings, Isaiah speaks out against the moral corruption around him. As he witnesses the defeat of the northern kingdom at the hands of the Assyrians, he knows that the destruction of Judah is also near. Yet through the bleakness, Isaiah proclaims God's promises.

Isaiah emphasizes the traditions concerning Zion, focusing on the permanence of Jerusalem and its temple. He knows that Mount Zion is the place of God's dwelling and the source of God's teaching, so that "in the days to come" people from every nation will stream to the holy city. Then God's word will go forth from Jerusalem so that the nations will transform their weapons of war into instruments of peace.

In days to come,
The mountain of the LORD's house
shall be established as the highest mountain
and raised above the hills.
All nations shall stream toward it.
Many peoples shall come and say:
"Come, let us go up to the LORD's mountain,
to the house of the God of Jacob,
That he may instruct us in his ways,
and we may walk in his paths."
For from Zion shall go forth instruction,
and the word of the LORD from Jerusalem.
He shall judge between the nations,
and set terms for many peoples.
They shall beat their swords into plowshares
and their spears into pruning hooks;
One nation shall not raise the sword against another,
nor shall they train for war again. (Isa 2:2-4)

Isaiah also accentuates the traditions about King David, insisting that a king from the line of David will be the agent of God's peace.

> For a child is born to us, a son is given to us;
>     upon his shoulder dominion rests.
> They name him Wonder-Counselor, God-Hero,
>     Father-Forever, Prince of Peace.
> His dominion is vast
>     and forever peaceful,
> Upon David's throne, and over his kingdom,
>     which he confirms and sustains
> By judgment and justice,
>     both now and forever. (Isa 9:5-6)

Isaiah proclaims both disaster and optimism, threat and hope, to bring God's people to conversion of heart. Although God's people will experience a burning purgation, a "remnant" will survive the destruction to be the means of continuing the history of salvation. Israel will be like a tree so thoroughly burned that only a stump remains, "As with a terebinth or an oak / whose trunk remains when its leaves have fallen" (Isa 6:13). But the prophet adds, "Holy offspring is the trunk."

Isaiah prophesies that the stump is rooted in God's promises to Abraham, Moses, and David. Just as a tree that is brought low with an ax will shoot forth branches from its fallen trunk, so from the stump of Jesse (the father of King David) a shoot will sprout and blossom.

> But a shoot shall sprout from the stump of Jesse,
>     and from his roots a bud shall blossom.
> The spirit of the Lord shall rest upon him:
>     a spirit of wisdom and of understanding,
> A spirit of counsel and of strength,
>     a spirit of knowledge and of fear of the Lord,
>     and his delight shall be the fear of the Lord.
>     (Isa 11:1-3)

The stump speaks of the dreadful chastisement the people and the house of David will endure. But the budding shoot is Israel's ideal king, the future anointed one for whom God's people hope. This true and faithful king, the messiah, will be anointed with God's own spirit and lead his people to fulfill God's covenant.

Micah the prophet is a contemporary of Isaiah, prophesying during the rule of three Judean kings. Micah performs a role in the southern kingdom similar to that of Amos in the northern kingdom. He speaks out strongly for the rights of the oppressed and against social injustices. He foretells that the destruction Israel has experienced will soon come upon Judah. His warnings are directed to priests, judges, prophets, and kings as he prophesies that no amount of external worship is capable of saving Jerusalem because of the corruption, bribery, and injustice within. His words challenge and inspire the people of Jerusalem to stop focusing merely on ritual sacrifice and turn back to authentic covenant faith.

> With what shall I come before the Lord,
>     and bow before God most high?
> Shall I come before him with burnt offerings,
>     with calves a year old?
> Will the Lord be pleased with thousands of
>     rams,
>     with myriad streams of oil?
> Shall I give my firstborn for my crime,
>     the fruit of my body for the sin of my soul?
> You have been told, O mortal, what is good,
>     and what the Lord requires of you:
> Only to do justice and to love goodness,
>     and to walk humbly with your God.
>     (Mic 6:6-8)

What does covenant commitment entail? The requirement expected here is total commitment to God. The prophet ends with a confession of guilt on the part of God's people and a statement of trust that God will forgive them. Doing justice, loving goodness, and walking humbly expresses this trust and faithfulness based on the promises God made to their ancestors.

**The Prophet Jeremiah**

Jeremiah begins his ministry under the reign of Josiah as a zealous supporter of the king's reforms. But Josiah's early death leads the prophet to criticize the succeeding unfaithful kings and to rebuke the people of the nation. The prophet denounces them for the false security they place in the temple. "Do not put your trust in these deceptive words: 'The temple of the LORD! The temple of the LORD! The temple of the LORD!'" says Jeremiah (Jer 7:4). They wrongfully place their trust in the temple of God rather than in the God of the temple.

> Only if you thoroughly reform your ways and your deeds; if each of you deals justly with your neighbor; if you no longer oppress the alien, the orphan, and the widow; if you no longer shed innocent blood in this place or follow after other gods to your own harm, only then will I let you continue to dwell in this place, in the land I gave your ancestors long ago and forever. (Jer 7:5-7)

The prophet argues that God destroyed the sacred shrine at Shiloh because of the sins of the people. There is no reason that God will not, for the same reasons, destroy the holy temple in Jerusalem. Jeremiah's words are considered blasphemous, and he is threatened with death.

We know more about the life of Jeremiah than any other prophet, thanks to the numerous biographical sections included in his prophetic book. From his call in his youth to the end of his life when Jerusalem is in ruin, Jeremiah suffers greatly through imprisonment, scourging, and plotting on his life. Often near despair, he gives us the clearest insights into the cost of prophetic ministry.

Despite the severe gloom of Jeremiah's oracles, his life is also characterized by an unquenchable hope. God's promise to use Jeremiah "to build and to plant" and the prophet's land purchase shows that beyond the destruction and the years of exile in Babylon, God will bring the people out of captivity and restore both Israel and Judah. With a new exodus, God will forgive his people and make with them a new covenant.

> See, days are coming—oracle of the LORD—when I will make a new covenant with the house of Israel and the house of Judah. It will

not be like the covenant I made with their ancestors the day I took them by the hand to lead them out of the land of Egypt. They broke my covenant, though I was their master—oracle of the LORD. But this is the covenant I will make with the house of Israel after those days—oracle of the LORD. I will place my law within them, and write it upon their hearts; I will be their God, and they shall be my people. They will no longer teach their friends and relatives, "Know the LORD!" Everyone, from least to greatest, shall know me—oracle of the LORD—for I will forgive their iniquity and no longer remember their sin. (Jer 31:31-34)

But during the last days of Jerusalem, this hope burns dim. The last king of Judah continues to fight against the Babylonians. After Jerusalem endures a long siege and severe famine, the enemy breaches the walls of Jerusalem, enters the city, and burns the temple to the ground in 587 BC. The king and the remainder of his army escape into the wilderness, but they are captured near Jericho. The king's sons are slain, and the king is blinded and brought to Babylon in chains. By the rivers of Babylon, God's people wait in captivity for the continuation of the drama of salvation.

---

With Babylon's defeat of Judah, the story of God's salvation in the land moves in reverse. The narrative began as God led Joshua and the people to Jericho, where they won a great victory through prayer and trust in God. But by ignoring God's word the king and people lose the land that God has promised through Abraham, Isaac, and Jacob. As the survivors among God's people travel eastward to Babylon, they move further away from the Promised Land and closer to the place where Abraham began his journey. God's people are now captive in Abraham's ancient homeland. All that God has done for Israel, beginning with Abraham's call, to Moses, Joshua, David, and Solomon, now seems lost as the people wait in exile by the rivers of Babylon.

These messages of the preexilic prophets are characterized by warning about the things to come. Consumed with a passion for right and justice they challenge the times in which they live. But in the exilic and postexilic prophets, which we will survey next, we see an increasing orientation toward the future and an irrepressible hope about the good things that await the people of God.

 The concern of Israel's prophets for the poor and vulnerable is a central part of the overarching theme of Scripture recognizing the **dignity of every person** and **God's special love for the poor**. This theme is amplified in the New Testament with the ministry of Jesus (Matt 25:31-46; Mark 1:40-42; Luke 4:18-21) and the church's ongoing commitment to the poor (Acts 11:27-30; Gal 2:10; Jas 2). Over time, in papal and episcopal documents grounded in Scripture, the church has developed a body of thought known as Catholic Social Teaching. These teachings insist upon basic principles of dignity and justice such as each person's right to life and work; our responsibility to take care of each other no matter our social status, religion or nationality; and care for the poor as a vital priority of society. In these and other principles of Catholic Social Teaching, prophets such as Amos and Isaiah continue to speak to our world.

## HOPING IN THE FUTURE

During the period of the exile, the prophets speak words of hope to the remnant of God's people in the midst of a situation that seems so hopeless. Jeremiah speaks God's word from Jerusalem to the exiles in Babylon: "For I know well the plans I have in mind for you—oracle of the LORD—plans for your welfare and not for woe, so as to give you a future of hope" (Jer 29:11). Jeremiah is speaking about the future that will soon come, when God's people will be freed from their captivity and return to Je-

rusalem. Yet he is also speaking about the broad horizon of God's promises, which will continue into the more distant future.

The exile provokes a crisis of faith for the people of Judah. The most foundational elements of God's covenant seem to have been destroyed. First, the kings of Judah are supposed to continue forever in the line of David. But now the Davidic monarchy seems to be at an end. Second, the land of Israel is supposed to be the dwelling of God's people. But now the land is in the possession of foreigners. Third, the temple is supposed to be the visible sign of God's presence with his people. Now, the temple stands in ruin and the priesthood and sacrifices no longer function.

Is God faithful to the promises made of old, or not? Has God forsaken Israel after all? Has the sin of Israel been too great to retain the covenant and the blessings promised? Beyond the disaster, the prophets see hope for the future, and they express that hope in many and varied ways.

### Ezekiel, the First Prophet of the Exile

Ezekiel is the first prophet to receive his call outside the land of Israel. A few years before the destruction of Jerusalem and the final defeat of God's people, he is taken into Babylon with the first wave of exiles. As a priest he would have lived his life in temple service and sacrifice. Yet God has called him to be a prophet. In a dramatic vision described at the beginning of his prophetic book, Ezekiel is commanded to eat the scroll of God's word and then to speak that word in a time of great crisis.

The book of his prophecy can be conveniently divided into two parts. The first consists of warnings and woes as he prepares the people for the destruction of Jerusalem and its temple. The second consists of prophecies given after the destruction. The prophet helps the people in exile understand that their calamity occurred not because the gods of Babylon are stronger but as just punishment for their sin. Nevertheless, the oracles and visions given in the final chapters are filled with words of promise and hope.

Ezekiel knows that those in exile are the hope for Israel's restoration. God will reestablish them in the land, not for their own sake, but for the sake of God's holy name which Israel has desecrated among the nations. God will rescue his people so that the other peoples of the world will see that he is the LORD: "Then the nations shall know that I am the LORD— oracle of the Lord GOD—when through you I show my holiness before their very eyes" (Ezek 36:23). In the face of the people's unworthiness, Israel's restoration will demonstrate God's noble generosity.

God will gather the dispersed people together, purify them of their defilement, and reestablish them as God's people. Cleansed and renewed, they will be given new hearts and God will put his own spirit within them.

I will take you away from among the nations, gather you from all the lands, and bring you back to your own soil. I will sprinkle clean water over you to make you clean; from all your impurities and from all your idols I will cleanse you. I will give you a new heart, and a new spirit I will put within you. I will remove the heart of stone from your flesh and give you a heart of flesh. I will put my spirit within you so that you walk in my statutes, observe my ordinances, and keep them. (Ezek 36:24-27)

The restoration of God's people is also depicted in Ezekiel's vision of the dry bones. God leads the prophet out to a broad valley that is filled with bones. God asks his prophet, "Can these bones come back to life?" God commands Ezekiel to speak the word of the LORD to them. As he speaks, the bones are brought to life in two stages: first, the bones are joined into skeletons and covered with sinews, flesh, and skin; then the life-giving breath comes into the corpses to make them live.

Thus says the Lord GOD to these bones: Listen! I will make breath enter you so you may come to life. I will put sinews on you, make flesh grow over you, cover you with skin, and put breath into you so you may come to life. Then you shall know that I am the LORD. I prophesied as I had been commanded. A sound started up, as I was prophesying, rattling like thunder. The bones came together, bone joining to bone. As I watched, sinews appeared on them, flesh grew over them, skin covered them on top, but there was no breath in them. Then he said to me: Prophesy to the breath, prophesy, son of man! Say to the breath: Thus says the Lord GOD: From the four winds come, O breath, and breathe into these slain that they may come to life. I prophesied as he commanded me, and the breath entered them; they came to life and stood on their feet, a vast army. He said to me: Son of man, these bones are the whole house of Israel! They are saying, "Our bones are dried up, our hope is lost, and we are cut off." Therefore, prophesy and say to them: Thus says the Lord GOD: Look! I am going to open your graves; I will make you come up out of your graves, my people, and bring you back to the land of Israel. You shall know that I am the LORD, when I open your graves and make you come up out of them, my people! I will put my spirit in you that you may come to life, and I will settle you in your land. Then you shall know that I am the LORD. I have spoken; I will do it—oracle of the LORD. (Ezek 37:5-14)

The scene is reminiscent of the primal act of creation when God formed the human person from the ground and breathed into that body the breath/wind/spirit of life (Gen 2:7). The same *ruah* (Hebrew: breath, wind, or spirit) of God causes the valley of bones to become a vast, living multitude. God is offering a new heart, a new spirit, a new covenant, and indeed a new creation rising from the ruins of the old.

With this new creation, the three foundational elements of God's covenant with Israel will be restored and renewed. First, the kingship in David's line will rule over all God's people. God says, "David my servant shall be king over them; they shall all have one shepherd" (Ezek 37:24). Second, the land will be returned to God's people. God says, "They shall live on the land I gave to Jacob my servant, the land where their ancestors lived; they shall live on it always" (Ezek 37:25). And third, the holy sanctuary of God's dwelling will be among them forever. God says, "My dwelling shall be with them; I will be their God, and they will be my people. Then the nations shall know that I, the LORD, make Israel holy, by putting my sanctuary among them forever" (Ezek 37:27-28).

This first prophet of the exile demonstrates that the exile marks an ending and a new beginning. It is a time of death and of re-creation. The task of the prophet is to proclaim the new ways God is acting in history, yet, at the same time, to assure Israel that the new is always rooted in and grows out of the old. Ezekiel is steeped in the tradition of the community's experience of God, but he is also prepared to preach a new way of living and being the people of God. Because God's people can remember the past, they have confidence that God can and will act in the future.

## A Prophetic Message of Comfort, Compassion, and Hope

As the exile is ending, a new prophet arises who continues in the prophetic spirit of Isaiah. The oracles of this prophet are referred to as Deutero-Isaiah or Second Isaiah, comprising chapters 40–55 of the book of Isaiah. These prophetic oracles keep the message of Isaiah alive and interpret it in Israel's new situation. Knowing that Israel's restoration is near, the message of this prophet is one of great comfort and optimism. The prophet speaks of the return from exile as a new exodus. The prophet realizes that the exodus is not just an event from the distant past, but always the pattern for the future. He begins his book of consolation with God's command to speak a message of comfort, compassion, and hope to a weary people.

Comfort, give comfort to my people,
  says your God.
Speak to the heart of Jerusalem, and proclaim
  to her
  that her service has ended,
  that her guilt is expiated,
That she has received from the hand of the LORD
  double for all her sins.

A voice proclaims:
In the wilderness prepare the way of the LORD!
  Make straight in the wasteland a highway
    for our God!
Every valley shall be lifted up,
  every mountain and hill made low;
The rugged land shall be a plain,
  the rough country, a broad valley.
Then the glory of the LORD shall be revealed,
  and all flesh shall see it together;
  for the mouth of the LORD has spoken.
    (Isa 40:1-5)

The time of God's judgment has ended; God is ready to act in a new and wondrous way. God who has made great promises to Israel in the past can be trusted to fulfill those promises in new ways. For as the prophet says: "The grass withers, the flower wilts, / but the word of our God stands forever" (Isa 40:8).

Couched within these prophecies of comfort and hope, Deutero-Isaiah speaks about a chosen Servant of God whom God will anoint with his spirit to bring justice to the nations. The Servant will be a light to the nations to bring God's salvation to the ends of the earth. The Servant is a man of suffering—beaten, disgraced, and spurned by others. Yet his innocent suffering is for the sake of his people.

Yet it was our pain that he bore,
  our sufferings he endured.
We thought of him as stricken,
  struck down by God and afflicted,
But he was pierced for our sins,
  crushed for our iniquity.
He bore the punishment that makes us whole,
  by his wounds we were healed.
We had all gone astray like sheep,
  all following our own way;
But the LORD laid upon him
  the guilt of us all. (Isa 53:4-6)

Despite the painful suffering that the Servant endures, the passage concludes in triumph:

Because of his anguish he shall see the light;
  because of his knowledge he shall be content;
My servant, the just one, shall justify the many,
  their iniquity he shall bear.

Therefore I will give him his portion among the
many,
and he shall divide the spoils with the
mighty,
Because he surrendered himself to death,
was counted among the transgressors,
Bore the sins of many,
and interceded for the transgressors.
(Isa 53:11-12)

For the prophet, the Servant may be a col-
lective image for the suffering people of Israel.
The image may also be that of a prophet or a
king who suffers to bring salvation to his
people. Certainly the figures of Moses and Jeremiah would come to mind from the past. The
Servant figure combines the best qualities of
the prophets, priests, and kings, and the Servant becomes the ideal Israelite who gives
shape to the people's future mission. The deliverance and redemption of God's people are
not without great price. But once the price is
paid, the blessings experienced by God's
people are limitless and unending.

### Prophecy after the Exile

With the decree of Cyrus, king of Persia, the
people in exile return to the land and look
upon the ruins of the city of Jerusalem. The first
of the postexilic prophets is Haggai. He sees
the discouragement of the people and urges
them to begin working on the new temple in
earnest. Haggai proclaims that the future
temple will be greater than the former. It will
be filled with God's glory, and there God will
extend *shalom*, the fullness of peace.

Greater will be the glory of this house
the latter more than the former—says the
LORD of hosts;
And in this place I will give you peace—
oracle of the LORD of hosts. (Hag 2:9)

Haggai also stirs up hope for an immediate
restoration of the line of David. The people
expect the kingship to be reestablished with
Zerubbabel, who served as governor over the
restored Judah after the exile. Yet after the days
of Zerubbabel, hope for an immediate restoration of the Davidic line quickly dies. But other
voices in the prophetic tradition continued to
keep alive Israel's yearning for a king in the
line of David.

The prophecy of Zechariah also encourages
the returning exiles and promotes the work of
rebuilding the temple. He speaks of "signs of
things to come"—namely, "my servant the
Branch" (Zech 3:8), the prophetic image for the
messiah from the line of David. The book contains symbolic visions of the renewed Jerusalem as a religious center, not just for Israel
but for all people, honored even by foreign
nations as the place of God's dwelling.

Many peoples and strong nations will come
to seek the LORD of hosts in Jerusalem and to
implore the favor of the LORD.
Thus says the LORD of hosts:
In those days ten people from nations of
every language will take hold, yes, will take
hold of the cloak of every Judahite and say,
"Let us go with you, for we have heard that
God is with you." (Zech 8:22-23)

This reminder of the universal mission of
Israel in the coming days of the messiah gives
hope to the returned exiles as they begin their
work of rebuilding. Although they seemed to
be a curse among the nations, God will make
them a blessing. What seems impossible for the
remnant of God's people will be brought about
by God. In the coming days, Jerusalem will be
a holy and faithful city where God will dwell
and to which people of every nation will want
to come.

The prophet Malachi speaks out several
years after Israel's return from exile. The
temple has been rebuilt, but routine and ne-
glect has set in. The community of faith seems
to be disintegrating, so Malachi calls the people
back to fidelity to the covenant. His preaching
leads the way for the reforms of Ezra and Nehemiah, which we spoke about in the historical
books.

In the closing chapter of the Old Testament,
we hear the words of Malachi:

Now I am sending my messenger—
  he will prepare the way before me;
And the lord whom you seek will come
  suddenly to his temple;
The messenger of the covenant whom you desire—
  see, he is coming! says the LORD of hosts.
    (Mal 3:1)

Although Malachi was not the final book of the Old Testament to be written, it is fitting that this book has been placed last since it recalls the ancient covenant and looks forward to the future fulfillment of that covenant.

The postexilic prophecies of Isaiah, chapters 56–66, are known as Trito-Isaiah or Third Isaiah. These prophecies in the spirit of Isaiah help God's people to understand why salvation has not yet come, and they encourage hope that God will intervene in a wondrous way in the future. After the great hopes following the exile have been shattered by the grim reality of life in Judah, they proclaim that God will do something astonishingly new.

One of the most encouraging oracles offers hope for a restored Jerusalem in which lasting peace will reign. The prophet proclaims a future that God will create anew.

See, I am creating new heavens
  and a new earth;
The former things shall not be remembered
  nor come to mind.
Instead, shout for joy and be glad forever
  in what I am creating.
Indeed, I am creating Jerusalem to be a joy
  and its people to be a delight;
I will rejoice in Jerusalem
  and exult in my people. (Isa 65:17-19)

Throughout the Bible God is always making things new, leading people to fuller and deeper experiences of salvation. God leads them from the covenant, relating to them with love and with mutual obligations, to the *new* covenant. God guides them from an experience of the temple in Jerusalem, promising to dwell with them there, to the *new* temple and the *new* Jerusalem. And God directs them from a creation marred by evil, sin, and death, to a *new* creation and, indeed, *new* heavens and a *new* earth.

Yet, throughout this period, God's people realize that their hopes for a new covenant with God, for a new king in the line of David, for a restored land, and for a renewed temple have been fulfilled only in a partial way. In fact, the words of the prophets are fulfilled in ways that are mediocre and far less than satisfying. The magnificent future expressed by the prophets is nowhere to be seen. Israel's hope is deferred but not abandoned.

## Apocalyptic Prophecy

As postexilic prophecy became increasingly future-oriented and universalized, it began to take on the characteristics of what is called "apocalyptic." We see the first manifestations of apocalyptic preaching in the postexilic prophetic books, with apocalyptic becoming a fully developed literary form in about 200 BC.

Apocalyptic literature is marked by several characteristics:

- it originates in a time of crisis in order to inspire hope;

- it is marked by confidence that God will destroy evil and reward the faithful with God's kingdom;

- it describes disturbances in the heavens and on the earth heralding the coming of the "day of the LORD"; and

- it uses symbolic names, numbers, and creatures to convey its message.

Some of the early development of the apocalyptic style can be seen in the strange symbolism of the prophet Ezekiel. Apocalyptic form can also be seen in parts of the books of Isaiah and Zechariah. But a more developed form of apocalyptic is seen in the prophet Joel, in whom we see a clear transition from prophetic to apocalyptic.

The prophecy of Joel is prompted by a terrible plague of locusts that make life miserable for the people. Joel tells the priests and the people to return to God with their whole heart, with prayer, and with fasting. Then Joel moves to apocalyptic language as he describes the plague as a symbol of the "day of the LORD." God's judgment will come upon all the nations, accompanied by dramatic disturbances in the heavens. As God's judgment falls on the nations, God brings salvation to his faithful ones.

God's coming redemption will bring a more inclusive community, breaking down the boundaries set up between people. Joel proclaims that God's *ruah*, which had previously been given to chosen judges, kings, and prophets, now will be bestowed on all, breaking the barriers of gender (sons and daughters), age (old and young), and social status (even servants and handmaids). God declares that the gifts of God's spirit will be poured out on all people.

> It shall come to pass
> I will pour out my spirit upon all flesh.
> Your sons and daughters will prophesy,
> your old men will dream dreams,
> your young men will see visions.
> Even upon your male and female servants,
> in those days, I will pour out my spirit.
> I will set signs in the heavens and on the earth,
> blood, fire, and columns of smoke;
> The sun will darken,
> the moon turn blood-red,
> Before the day of the LORD arrives,
> that great and terrible day.
> Then everyone who calls upon the name of the
> LORD
> will escape harm.
> For on Mount Zion there will be a remnant,
> as the LORD has said,
> And in Jerusalem survivors
> whom the LORD will summon. (Joel 3:1-5)

The one Old Testament book that reveals all the characteristics of apocalyptic literature is Daniel. It is named for its hero, who is said to live among the exiles in Babylon. It was put in its present form in the second century at the time of Antiochus IV and his persecution of the Jews. The stories of Daniel show how God saves those who are faithful in times of persecution.

The accounts of the three young men in the fiery furnace, Daniel in the lion's den, and Daniel's interpretation of the handwriting on the wall are meant to be instructive and encouraging. The stories of Daniel's life in Babylon could be easily applied to the Jews undergoing persecution in about 165 BC, offering them confidence and hope in their trials. Those who trust in God and are faithful in times of trial are preserved from harm.

The apocalyptic messages are represented in a series of dreams and visions. The dream of the Babylonian king presents the progression of world empires as a frightening statue made up of various metals: the head of gold, chest and arms of silver, belly and thighs of bronze, and legs of iron with its feet mixed with clay. In the dream, a stone is hewn from a mountain without a hand being put to it. The stone strikes the feet and the whole statue crumbles at once and is blown away by the wind. The stone, however becomes a great mountain that fills the whole earth.

Daniel interprets the dream for the Babylonian king. He is the head of gold whose empire will be followed by inferior kingdoms. He explains that the stone crushing the statue is the eternal kingdom of God.

> In the lifetime of those kings the God of heaven will set up a kingdom that shall never be destroyed or delivered up to another people; rather, it shall break in pieces all these kingdoms and put an end to them, and it shall stand forever. That is the meaning of the stone you saw hewn from the mountain without a hand being put to it, which broke in pieces the iron, bronze, clay, silver, and gold. The great God has revealed to the king what shall be in the future; this is exactly what you dreamed, and its meaning is sure. (Dan 2:44-45)

In another vision, Daniel sees four terrifying beasts that come from the sea. These, too, represent four successive empires holding God's people captive. Daniel continues to describe his visions as he sees a figure coming on the clouds who will reign forever.

As the visions during the night continued, I saw coming with the clouds of heaven

> One like a son of man.
> When he reached the Ancient of Days
>   and was presented before him,
> He received dominion, splendor, and kingship;
>   all nations, peoples and tongues will serve him.
> His dominion is an everlasting dominion
>   that shall not pass away,
>   his kingship, one that shall not be
>     destroyed. (Dan 7:13-14)

This "son of man" figure represents the people of God, those whom Daniel calls "the holy ones of the Most High." These are the ones who hold fast to their faith in spite of the persecutions they must endure. "The Ancient of Days" is, of course, a title for the LORD. God takes dominion away from the rulers of the earth and presents it to the "one like a son of man." He represents the eternal kingdom of God that cannot be destroyed.

Daniel's dreams and visions describe the period between the earthly kingdoms and the coming kingdom of God. Jewish tradition refers to this as the period of tribulation or the time of the birth pangs of the messiah. After the suffering is endured, the age of fulfillment—the age of the Messiah—will dawn.

## The Coming of the Messiah

As we look at the entire sweep of Israel's prophetic tradition, we realize that prophecies take on fuller meanings in later ages—meanings that go far beyond the original significance of the prophet's words. While individual prophets spoke out in the midst of their own historical situation, later authors interpret their words in light of their fuller understanding of God's plan. For example, when Nathan prophesied that the kingdom of David would last forever, he could not have imagined the full significance of those words for God's people. Yet later ages are able to see how that covenant with David is part of God's whole plan for the coming of the messiah and the realization of God's kingdom.

With the coming of each new king, the hopes of God's people flame anew. Isaiah hopes for the birth of the Prince of Peace, the great light that will shine upon Israel. Jeremiah foretells the new covenant and the new David who will govern wisely and bring justice to the land. Ezekiel describes a new temple in which the LORD will be present forever and the new spirit that will fill God's people. Daniel describes the coming of one like a Son of Man whose reign will be worldwide and everlasting.

As king after king fails to live up to the hopes placed in him, as the anointed priests and temple fail to mediate God's blessings, and as the peace and blessings of the covenant are not realized, God's people and prophets look more and more toward God's future intervention. They know that God's word is eternal and God's promises are unconditional, but they also know that historical Israel is unable to bring about God's reign and salvation over the world. The words and images of the prophets increasingly awaken God's people to the power of God acting beyond Israel's immediate reality and involving the whole world.

Through periods of Israel's suffering, the prophetic imagery speaks about a humble, suffering one who will fulfill God's promises. Zechariah foretells a saving king, who comes not in glory but in humility: "Exult greatly, O daughter Zion! / Shout for joy, O daughter Jerusalem! / Behold, your king is coming to you / a just savior is he, / Humble, and riding on a donkey" (Zech 9:9). His dominion will be worldwide and he will proclaim peace to the nations. In another image, a suffering one who has been pierced becomes the means of divine blessings for the family of David and the people of Jerusalem: "When they look on him whom they have thrust through, they will mourn for him as one mourns for an only child" (Zech 12:10).

Deutero-Isaiah speaks about a chosen Servant of God whom God will anoint with his spirit to bring justice to the nations. The light to all the nations and to the ends of the earth will also be a man of suffering—beaten, disgraced, and spurned by others—who is "pierced for our sins, / crushed for our iniquity" (Isa 53:5).

As the centuries pass and the Babylonian captivity is only a distant memory, the people of God continue to experience a sense of continuing exile. Their hopes, expressed in the writings of the prophets, include God's return to dwell among his people, the establishment of God's worldwide reign and restoration of creation, and the renewal of hearts to live God's covenant in a new and radical way. When these hopes are realized, the story of Israel will be brought to a satisfying and wondrous conclusion.

Israel's ancient Scriptures lead God's people to messianic expectations rooted in the royal, priestly, and prophetic traditions. This developing anticipation of the messiah is rich and diverse, with its roots in a variety of perspectives. Yet each strain of expectancy focuses on a divinely chosen individual who will bring the whole world into a full and lasting relationship with God and with God's saving power.

---

As we conclude this section of the biblical panorama, we realize that the Scriptures are a vast treasure chest. Every person, story, event, poem, and prophetic oracle in the Old Testament has great value in itself. Yet, stepping back and seeing the broad picture, we realize that through it all, God has always acted with a single unified plan for human history. Through it all, the promises made to Abraham are being fulfilled—all the nations of the earth will be blessed through him.

The people of God have never looked upon written revelation as a lifeless record from the past, but always as something oriented toward the future. Earlier events of our salvation help us to understand later events more fully. The Old Testament was the faith heritage of Jesus and is a necessary part of the heritage of every Christian. No Christian can understand the revelation of the New Testament without delving into the rich understanding of God given to us through the Scriptures of the people of Israel. This book of Israel is also the book of the church.

By reading the stories of our ancestors in faith, we know who we are, where we come from, and where we are going. We learn the truths that keep our family of faith together, and we learn how we are to live as members of the family of God.

From its earliest days, the church has found the person of **Jesus Christ foreshadowed** and present in the Old Testament. In Luke's account of the encounter of the risen Christ with some of his disciples on the road to Emmaus, Luke writes, "Then beginning with Moses and all the prophets, he [Jesus] interpreted to them what referred to him in all the scriptures" (Luke 24:27; see also John 5:39). Of course, "the scriptures" here refers to what we now call the Old Testament. The *Catechism of the Catholic Church* explains the connection between the Old and New Testaments in this way: "The unity of the two Testaments proceeds from the unity of God's plan and his Revelation. The Old Testament prepares for the New and the New Testament fulfills the Old; the two shed light on each other; both are true Word of God" (140).

## EXPLORING LESSON FOUR

1. What is the role of a prophet in Israel? How does the prophetic message relate to the past, the present, and the future?

_____

_____

_____

_____

2. What is the difference between a true prophet and a false prophet?

_____

_____

_____

_____

3. The prophetic books tell several stories of God calling reluctant or utterly unprepared prophets. Has God ever called you to do something you did not want to do or did not feel prepared to do? How did you respond?

_____

_____

_____

_____

4. What are the two major themes of the prophets? How are they related to each other? (For examples, see Hos 4:1-3; Amos 5:7-14; Micah 6:8-10.)

_____

_____

_____

_____

5. What is one thing in particular that stands out for you (or something new that you learned) from the accounts of the prophetic ministries of Amos, Hosea, Isaiah, Micah, and Jeremiah?

_____

_____

_____

_____

_____

6. Describe the "crisis of faith" that resulted from the Babylonian exile. What was the central message of the prophets of this time in response to this crisis?

_____

_____

_____

_____

_____

7. How did "apocalyptic prophecy" help to maintain Israel's hope during a time of ongoing oppression and disappointment?

_____

_____

_____

_____

_____

8. What are some reasons why hope for a Messiah escalated in the centuries before the birth of Jesus?

_____

_____

_____

_____

_____

9. Reflect on your experience of learning more about the Old Testament. What knowledge have you found most valuable? How would you describe the value of the Old Testament for Christians?

_____

_____

_____

_____

_____

**CLOSING PRAYER**

*Prayer*

*Yet just as from the heavens
   the rain and snow come down
And do not return there
   till they have watered the earth,
   making it fertile and fruitful,
Giving seed to the one who sows
   and bread to the one who eats,
So shall my word be
   that goes forth from my mouth;
It shall not return to me empty,
   but shall do what pleases me,
   achieving the end for which I sent it.*
      (Isa 55:10-11)

Lord our God, your word has gone forth and has come to rest with your people. May it find fertile ground in our hearts and in our lives so that it never returns to you empty. Teach us to value your word in all of its richness, history and diversity. And now we pray for those who are most in need of your rich love, especially . . .

# PRAYING WITH YOUR GROUP

Because we know that the Bible allows us to hear God's voice, prayer provides the context for our study and sharing. By speaking and listening to God and each other, the discussion often grows to more deeply bond us to one another and to God.

At *the beginning and end of each lesson* simple prayers are provided for individual use, and also may be used within the group setting. Most of the closing prayers provided with each lesson relate directly to a theme from that lesson and encourage you to pray together for people and events in your local community.

Of course, there are many ways to center ourselves in God's presence as we gather together in groups around the word of God. We provide some additional suggestions here knowing you and your group will make prayer a priority as part of your gathering. These are simply alternative ways to pray if your group would like to try something different from those prayers provided in the previous pages.

## Conversational Prayer

This form of prayer allows for the group members to pray in their own words in a way that is not intimidating. The group leader begins with Step One, inviting all to focus on the presence of Christ among them. After a few moments of quiet, the group leader invites anyone in the group to voice a prayer or two of thanksgiving; once that is complete, then anyone who has personal intentions may pray in their own words for their needs; finally, the group prays for the needs of others.

A suggested process:
In your own words, speak simple and short prayers to allow time for others to add their voices.

Focus on one "step" at a time, not worrying about praying for everything in your mental list at once.

| | |
|---|---|
| Step One | Visualize Christ. Welcome him. |
| | Imagine him present with you in your group. |
| | Allow time for some silence. |
| Step Two | Gratitude opens our hearts. |
| | Use simple words such as, "Thank you, Lord, for . . ." |
| Step Three | Pray for your own needs knowing that others will pray with you. |
| | Be specific and honest. |
| | Use "I" and "me" language. |

| Step Four | Pray for others by name, with love. |
|---|---|
| | You may voice your agreement ("Yes, Lord"). |
| | End with gratitude for sharing concerns. |

## Praying Like Ignatius

St. Ignatius Loyola, whose life and ministry are the foundation of the Jesuit community, invites us to enter into Scripture texts in order to experience the scenes, especially scenes of the gospels or other narrative parts of Scripture. Simply put, this is a method of creatively imagining the scene, viewing it from the inside, and asking God to meet you there. Most often, this is a personal form of prayer, but in a group setting, some of its elements can be helpful if you allow time for this process.

A suggested process:

- Select a scene from the chapters in the particular lesson.
- Read that scene out loud in the group, followed by some quiet time.
- Ask group members to place themselves in the scene (as a character, or as an onlooker) so that they can imagine the emotions, responses, and thinking that may have taken place. Notice the details and the tone, and imagine the interaction with the Lord that is taking place.
- Share with the group any insights that came to you in this quiet imagining.
- Allow each person in the group to thank God for some insight and to pray about some request that may have surfaced.

## Sacred Reading (or Lectio Divina)

This method of prayer invites us to "listen with the ear of the heart" as St. Benedict's rule would say. We listen to the words and the phrasing, asking God to speak to our innermost being. Again, this method of prayer is most often used in an individual setting but may also be used in an adapted way within a group.

A suggested process:

- Select a scene from the chapters in the particular lesson.
- Read the scene out loud in the group, perhaps two times.
- Ask group members to ponder a word or phrase that stands out to them.
- The group members could then simply speak the word or phrase as a kind of litany of what was meaningful for your group.
- Allow time for more silence to ponder the words that were heard, asking God to reveal to you what message you are meant to hear, how God is speaking to you.
- Follow up with spoken intentions at the close of this group time.

# REFLECTING ON SCRIPTURE

Reading Scripture is an opportunity not simply to learn new information but to listen to God who loves you. Pray that the same Holy Spirit who guided the formation of Scripture will inspire you to correctly understand what you read, and empower you to make what you read a part of your life.

The inspired word of God contains layers of meaning. As you make your way through passages of Scripture, whether studying a book of the Bible or focusing on a biblical theme, you may find it helpful to ask yourself these four questions:

*What does the Scripture passage say?*
Read the passage slowly and reflectively. Become familiar with it. If the passage you are reading is a narrative, carefully observe the characters and the plot. Use your imagination to picture the scene or enter into it.

*What does the Scripture passage mean?*
Read the footnotes in your Bible and the commentary provided to help you understand what the sacred writers intended and what God wants to communicate by means of their words.

*What does the Scripture passage mean to me?*
Meditate on the passage. God's word is living and powerful. What is God saying to you? How does the Scripture passage apply to your life today?

*What am I going to do about it?*
Try to discover how God may be challenging you in this passage. An encounter with God contains a challenge to know God's will and follow it more closely in daily life. Ask the Holy Spirit to inspire not only your mind but your life with this living word.